Merry Christmas to Susan Mary

December 25, 1982

With much love from Nancy Joy.

East Bergholt Old Hall, 1801. Oil on canvas, 28″ × 42″ (71 × 107 cm)
Courtauld Institute Galleries, London

THE DAYS OF BOYHOOD — 1776–1799

The River Stour rises in the quaintly named Gog Magog Hills, which form the eastern extension of the rather better-known Chilterns in that part of England called East Anglia. Beginning as a tiny, gurgling brook, the river flows gently eastward through a green and tranquil valley, joining briefly with the River Ouse before emptying its waters into the North Sea at the port of Harwich.

On the banks of this peaceful river sit several small, quiet villages, their gray and brown flint church steeples rising above picturesque eighteenth-century thatched cottages, and hedge-lined lanes leading out into some of the best farmland in England. Beyond this can be seen the rich green foliage of the mighty oaks, the elms and sycamore, ash and willow, stretching into the gently rising hills.

The area today is dependent primarily upon agriculture, as it was just over two hundred years ago when England was a peaceful land untroubled by war or strife. King George III was on the throne, a popular and fair monarch with, as yet, no signs of the disease which was to confine him to Windsor Castle as a madman early in the next century.

The American War of Independence, raging far across the Atlantic, was of very little interest to most people outside London, and the Declaration of Independence, signed on July 4, 1776, did virtually nothing to disturb the rural calm of a pleasant English summer.

Twenty-three days earlier, on a bright and warm Tuesday morning, June 11, in a house on the edge of the village of East Bergholt, Ann Constable experienced the joys and pains of childbirth for the fourth time. The baby — a boy — was weak and fragile, and was having considerable difficulty in breathing. As he was not expected to live for much longer than a day, the rector of East Bergholt parish church, the Reverend Mr. Driffield, was summoned to the house to baptize the boy. He was given the name of John.

The Constable family had originated in Yorkshire, but had begun to migrate southward sometime in the mid-seventeenth century when Hugh Constable, John's great-grandfather, had left the bleak Yorkshire moors for the flat, arable land around the village of Bures on the Essex-Suffolk border. Hugh worked long and hard on his farmland and made a successful start to his life in East Anglia. Encouraged by this, other members of the family followed him south. By 1774 Golding Constable, Hugh's grandson, was the owner of a thriving flour-milling business that included the water mills on the Stour at Flatford and Dedham and two windmills near East Bergholt. In that same year, he moved, with his wife and three young children, into their new house in that village. It was here that John Constable was born.

Contrary to the fears of both parents, John survived his first days and became a healthy, robust child who grew to love the Suffolk countryside. He delighted in watching the corn-laden barges being pulled along the canalized Stour by the powerful horses that plodded along the towpaths.

The earliest reminiscences of the young John Constable were of wide-open countryside, horse-drawn plows tilling the soil, golden harvests, the ever-changing canopy of cloud and sky above the land; and of the silvery river with its barges, horses, locks, and constant, yet unhurried, activity. Now, when we look at one of his magnificent landscapes, we are transported back two hundred years to the serenity of the agricultural society of eighteenth-century rural East Anglia. When he was seven years old he was sent to a boarding school at Lavenham, a small town some fourteen miles from East Bergholt. It was the custom in England at that time to send boys to a boarding school if their parents could afford it.

John's easygoing home life was suddenly shattered by an assistant master at Lavenham who delighted in regularly beating the boys on the most slender of pretexts. After only a month or so his parents became so aware of John's unhappiness that he was taken from the school and returned to the more sympathetic climate of home life, and enrolled as a day pupil at a school in the village of Dedham nearby. Here the Master, the Reverend Dr. Grimwood, was a far more tender and patient teacher who gently maneuvered his pupils through their lessons, persuading them rather than punishing.

John was a mediocre student — not brilliant, by any means — and he spent much of his time, according to Dr. Grimwood, daydreaming in a little world of his own. He was to remain at this school under the tender tutelage of Dr. Grimwood until he was seventeen.

At some time during his early teens John became friendly with the tenant of the cottage close to the front gate of East Bergholt House. The tenant, John Dunthorne, was six years older than Constable and was, by vocation, a glazier. Dunthorne himself was a fairly gifted amateur painter and he encouraged and instructed his young admirer in the basics of sketching and painting, often taking him along on sketching trips in the surrounding Suffolk countryside. Dunthorne was the earliest artistic influence on Constable and, despite the reticence of his parents to develop this friendship with a man from a lower social class, the relationship was of importance in whetting the boy's appetite for painting. Dunthorne was no «master,» but he did manage to generate in his willing pupil sufficient enthusiasm to release the talents latent within him.

By 1792 it had become fairly obvious to the Constable family that their son was not particularly interested in taking over the business of running the mills. Painting and sketching seemed to be taking up every minute of his spare time, his interest in milling dwindling conversely to his growing enthusiasm for art.

Aware of this, and anxious that her son's sole influence in art should not be confined to the village glazier, Mrs. Constable obtained for him an introduction to Sir George Beaumont, a truly gifted amateur painter, an art collector, and a man of high social standing. Sir George often used to visit his aged mother, the Dowager Lady Beaumont, who lived in a fine house in Dedham, and it was here that the young John Constable first met the man who was to become a lifelong friend and his patron. Some of the lad's sketches were shown to Sir George, who immediately recognized in them an undeveloped talent. He encouraged John to copy some of the great masters, and put several paintings at his disposal, including Claude's *Hagar and the Angel*. This magnificent painting, completed by the French artist in 1646, completely captivated young Constable, and, like the revelation on the road to Damascus, pointed his way forward. He resolved to become a painter.

CONSTABLE

Constable

by Peter D. Smith

CROWN PUBLISHERS, INC. - NEW YORK

Title page: JOHN CONSTABLE
by D. Maclise, 1831
Drawing, $5\frac{7}{8}'' \times 4\frac{1}{2}''$ (15 × 11.5 cm)
National Portrait Gallery, London

Collection published under the direction of:
MADELEINE LEDIVELEC-GLOECKNER

PHOTOGRAPHS

Documentation Photographique de la Réunion des Musées Nationaux, Paris – E. Dulière, Brussels – Lauros-Giraudon, Paris – Michael Marsland, New Haven, Connecticut – Joseph Szaszfai, New Haven, Connecticut – John Webb, London.

Library of Congress Cataloging in Publication Data
Smith, Peter D.
  Constable.

    1. Constable, John, 1776–1837.   I. Constable,
John, 1776–1837. II. Title.
ND497.C7S64   1981,   759.2   81–7758
ISBN 0–517–54428–8   AACR2

GIRL AND DOG IN A LANDSCAPE, 1789. Watercolor and pencil, $8^5/_8''\times 8^1/_{16}''$ (22.8 × 20.5 cm)
Private collection

Bridge at Haddon. Sketchbook, August 17, 1801
Pencil and sepia wash, 6¾" × 10⅛" (17.1 × 25.8 cm)
Victoria and Albert Museum, London

The Entrance to the Village of Edensor, 1801
Pencil and sepia wash, 6⅝″ × 10⅛″ (17 × 25.7 cm)
Victoria and Albert Museum, London

Another important influence on Constable at this time was George Frost, a senior clerk in the office of the Blue Coach Service, which operated between Ipswich and London. Frost, then about fifty, was also an amateur painter who used to spend much of his time seeking out the almost unchanged parts of Ipswich that Thomas Gainsborough had painted forty years earlier, and putting on them his own interpretation. Frost's talent and his kindly guidance were also an important early influence on Constable, though within a few years the pupil had outmastered his teacher.

In the summer of 1796, at the age of twenty, John Constable journeyed for the first time to London with his father on business, but stayed on for a while at the home of a maternal aunt in Edmonton. Certain introductions to people in the art world had been arranged for him in order that he might discuss whether the life of an artist was one he should pursue seriously. Among those he met was John Thomas Smith — affectionately known as «Antiquity» Smith — who had been born in a hackney carriage, had become an engraver, was, at the time, an art teacher at a school in Edmonton, and was to publish several books on art and antiques (his pet subjects, hence his name), later to become Keeper of Antiquities at the British Museum before dying a bankrupt in 1833. At the time of their meeting Smith was writing a book called «Remarks on Rural Scenery» and he encouraged Constable to send him pencil sketches of Suffolk scenes, to which the young man eagerly acquiesced. Some of these sketches still survive and are among the oldest known works of Constable.

A further influence upon the young aspirant at this time was John Cranach, a friend of Smith who happened to be in London at the time. Cranach was a Devon painter, and he encouraged Constable to buy books on art in order to read the remarks on the development of style of the masters and their technique; he also told Constable to study anatomy.

The influence and advice of these two London-based painters was of immense value to Constable for, unlike Sir George Beaumont, or the Suffolk George Frost and John Dunthorne, these two were professionals, hardened to the rigors of life in a difficult and highly competitive vocation. Their advice, therefore, was more practical than that of his early tutors. Smith even recommended that Constable return to Suffolk and take over his father's milling business which he pointed out, held out a much greater chance of success than the unpredictable world of art.

John returned home disillusioned — unsure of what to do. He desperately wanted to paint, yet was mature enough to recognize the dangers in giving up the opportunity to take over the business from his father. For a time he took Smith's advice, plunging himself into the affairs of milling and grinding corn, but he was still torn between the security of this sort of life and his love of painting.

His parents were aware of his deep concern, and, after a fairly lengthy family debate, it was decided that John should follow his heart's ambition and take further study to see if he really did have sufficient talent to become a full-time painter.

It must have proved a very difficult decision for we must remember that at this time painters lived almost solely from portrait commissions, and landscape painting as we know it today, which was John's main interest, did not exist at all; the only landscapes to be seen were the backgrounds for portraits or religious paintings.

It was, therefore, with a deep sense of foreboding, yet an unusual degree of selfless parental understanding, that Mr. and Mrs. Constable said goodbye to their son as he clambered aboard the London coach on February 3, 1799, bound for a probationary period of study at the Royal Academy, then based at Somerset House in the Strand.

THE YEARS OF LEARNING — 1799–1809

For a young man from the country London presented an almost frightening prospect — the glittering life of the West End, with its theaters and coffeehouses, the nearby hubbub of the City, with its banks, merchants' houses, and other institutions. The French Revolution had sent its tremors rippling across the Channel to be felt in the English capital, but did little to disturb the gay life of the dandies of the day — the eighteenth-century version of the jet set. George III was still king, though by now living at Windsor between bouts of madness, leaving the limelight to his son, the Prince of Wales (later to become George IV), who gathered round his glittering, but corpulent figure such people as the legendary Beau Brummell.

HEAD OF A GIRL IN PROFILE, c. 1806–1809. Oil on canvas, 12¼″ × 12″ (31.2 × 30.5 cm)
Victoria and Albert Museum, London

The march of Napoleon across the face of Europe did little to stint the gaiety of the Establishment who continued to spend lavishly on their material luxuries while the less fortunate were reduced to the state of poverty so aptly described by Charles Dickens some years later.

The Royal Academy was an integral part of the Establishment and was the self-appointed sole arbiter of the value of works of art. It had a virtual monopoly in the exhibition of paintings, and no artist could achieve lasting fame without the seal of approval of the Academy. Until this time Constable's main influences had been those of the men we have mentioned. His style was restricted to that of his mentors and lacked the freedom of self-confidence. His brushstrokes were hesitant, restrained, his colors muted.

Like most students at the Academy, he spent much time in copying from the great masters, and in drawing from life or from casts. His life drawing did not show any extraordinary talent, nor yet did his copies, although his work direct from nature did show just a hint of that genius which was later to reveal itself.

He lived quite simply, renting three rooms at number 50 Rathbone Place, just off Oxford Street. He was quite satisfied with this little abode, having one of the rooms looking out onto the street, with a large window which gave him excellent light in which to work. In the summer vacation of 1801 he set out on a tour of the Peak District of Derbyshire, with Daniel Whalley, the younger brother of his sister Martha's husband. It was during this trip that he met the poet Wordsworth for the first time, and although they did not become particularly enamored of each other, they did meet often in later years as both were to be patronized by Sir George Beaumont.

Constable did not make a lasting habit of the fairly normal artistic practice of undertaking regular summer sketching trips (apart from a few years in Suffolk, which we shall come to later), but the years in which he did make a summer journey have left us a remarkable record of his work. The sketchbook from this year, 1801, contains works in a variety of mediums: chalk, pencil, watercolor, and one or two oils. Although the influence of his mentors can be seen, his work at this time was just beginning to take on its own character. Faults can, of course, be found, and it is likely that these were pointed out to him by his tutors at the Royal Academy. The tone in many of his sketches does not appear to be true, and his understanding of shadow was not yet up to its later standard.

Sir George Beaumont's influence can also be seen in what was Constable's first commission — a painting of East Bergholt House for its owner, John Reade. Some of Constable's friends thought Sir George had painted in the trees in this picture. The sky, however, is clearly by Constable, with the high clouds, like a high ceiling in a room, giving a sense of space and light, and providing a marvelous backdrop to the long wide vista of the house itself. The picture is privately owned.

This painting was made during one of his many trips home to his beloved Suffolk, normally at vacation times, and we can imagine his joy as he rediscovered the freshness and calm of the countryside, so noticeable after the clamor of London. For anyone brought up in the country, cities can never seem clean or fresh, and even at the start of the nineteenth century London was full of pollution — not from the fumes of motor vehicles but from chimneys and the early industries. Constable was never entirely happy in the city, preferring the cleanliness and peace of East Anglia, and although he lived much of his adult life in the capital, he did so primarily to be near the center of artistic life. After all, prospective purchasers were far more numerous in London than in East Bergholt.

It was on one of these trips home that he decided to become a landscape painter or, as he put it to John Dunthorne in a letter written during the summer of 1802, « a natural painter. »

This statement is worth remembering for it indicates that he had, by the age of twenty-five, clearly made up his mind about the sort of life he wanted to lead. At the Academy he had, of course, studied all the facets of art — portraits, life drawing, still life, religious works, and the occasional landscape; but he had resolved that only one of these would provide him with the satisfaction he needed, and while he continued to paint portraits and other works, these were only a means to earn money.

His first exhibit at the Royal Academy Exhibition was shown in 1802. We can assume that he did submit one or two paintings the previous year but that these were rejected by the selection committee. Unfortunately, we can not be certain which painting Constable exhibited; the catalogues states only that a landscape was shown. It is possible that it was a view of Windsor, which he had visited earlier in the year, but it seems more likely that it was a painting of his beloved Suffolk and could have been the undated *Road near Dedham.** It was a view that Constable was to paint many times in his life, and it is thus

_____

* See p. 13.

ROAD NEAR DEDHAM, 1802. Oil on canvas, 13⅛″ × 16⅜″ (33.2 × 41.5 cm)
Yale Center for British Art, New Haven, Conn. Paul Mellon Collection

13

VIEW IN BORROWDALE, October 4, 1806
Pencil and watercolor, 7½″ × 10¾″ (19.1 × 27.4 cm)
Victoria and Albert Museum, London

◁
GIRL AT A WINDOW, 1806. Watercolor, 8″ × 7″ (20.5 × 17.8 cm)
Courtauld Institute Galleries, London

KESWICK LAKE, 1806. Oil on canvas, 10½″ × 17½″ (26.5 × 44.7 cm)
National Gallery of Victoria, Melbourne. Felton Bequest

worth examining together with some of the later versions to see just how much his technique developed over a period of thirty years. Eighteen hundred and two was also the year that he first painted Willy Lott's house, another Suffolk feature he was to return to time and time again.

In October of that year, while still at East Bergholt, he bought a small studio in one of the cottages close to his parents' home, and here he worked, intermittently, throughout the fall and winter, completing four landscapes that were to be shown at the next year's Academy exhibition, although here again, we are uncertain as to their exact identity.

In April of 1803, having delivered his paintings to the Academy, he embarked on a sea voyage, though not of any great length, for he only journeyed from London to Deal on the Kent coast. Although the trip was of a relatively short distance, it did take almost a month, giving him plenty of time to sketch the shipping while sailing down the Thames estuary, which was then the busiest shipping area in the British Isles. The vessel, the East Indiaman «Coutts» — the captain of which was an old friend of his father — put in at Gravesend for several days, giving Constable the opportunity to walk across the Kent hills to Chatham and Rochester. He drew the magnificent castle in the latter town, while, at Chatham, which was then a major naval port, he made a number of sketches of some of the British Navy's men-of-war lying at peaceful anchor in the still waters of the River Medway. Among them was the «Victory» later to rise to fame as the flagship of Admiral Nelson in the Battle of Trafalgar in 1805.

The continuation of the «Coutts» journey gave him further opportunities to sketch shipping, and he also had time to take an interest in cloud patterns. Being the son of a miller, he had always been alert to the vagaries of the weather, and although he did not make serious studies of cloud pattern and behavior until considerably later in his life, his interest in the effects of clouds can be said to date from this period. We have seen in his painting of East Bergholt House two years previously that he was aware of the effects of light and shadow cast by the clouds, but this trip down the blustery Thames was the first time he became interested in clouds as items in their own right. Of particular fascination to him was a major storm off the notorious North Foreland, which delayed the ship for three days. He managed to struggle out on deck to observe the Satanic clouds rolling past the heaving decks. He could not sketch the clouds then, as there was too much movement of the ship as it was tossed about, giant waves breaking over its wooden bows.

He left the «Coutts» at Deal, returning to London via Dover. Although, prior to disembarkation, he had taken the greatest care to protect his sketches from the weather and salt air, he found, on reaching the shore, that he had left them all on board! Fortunately, they were all returned to him, unharmed, when the ship docked after its long journey east in 1804.

On arrival in London, he went to the Academy Exhibition, where he saw some of Turner's works and was fairly critical of them, complaining to a friend that they seemed too extravagant and too far away from nature.

Turner, just a few months older than Constable, was, by this time, a full academician, a height to which Constable was not to aspire for another twenty-six years, and it is interesting to note the differences between them and the effect this had on Constable. Constable was, and always remained, the boy from the country; Turner, although not high-born, being the son of a barber, managed to ingratiate himself with those who had influence in society, and, from the age of fourteen, was patronized by well-known art collectors. Before he was twenty-eight he had a house in fashionable Harley Street, with his own studio and a permanent one-man exhibition, the first of its kind in England. As an Academician, he was entitled to exhibit as many works as he chose at the Exhibition, but preferred, after 1804, to use his own gallery as an outlet for his paintings.

Later in his life Turner was almost certainly partly responsible for witholding full Academy membership from Constable, for reasons we can only ponder. Certainly their styles were very different, with Constable being absorbed with, for example, the beauty of a tree, and Turner seeing only a mass of light and color. Their differing backgrounds may partly explain this disparity, for we must remember that Constable spent his youth wandering the Suffolk countryside, with its clear, fresh air and sunshine, whereas Turner was London born and bred, and spent his youth peering through the mists at the shipping on the Thames.

Constable's criticism of Turner's work was partly due to his inferiority complex, but was more, I think, the result of his different outlook on life, and on nature and its portrayal. This competitiveness between the two, which was not that amicable, was really quite a shame, for they are very complementary artists.

After staying for a few weeks in the capital, Constable went down to the Suffolk countryside for the rest of the summer, and spent a fair amount of time sketching in the company of his old friend George Frost. An interesting comparison is possible of their two styles, for on October 5 they sat next to each other on the banks of the River Orwell at Ipswich and completed watercolors of the shipping on the river and the warehouses on the opposite bank. The superior clarity and character of Constable's version are clearly perceptible. Although there are a few differences in the composition, which might indicate that they were both finished off later in the studio, the main points to compare are in the technical aspects. The boats in Frost's sketch do not appear to be in the water, but rather on it, while Constable's are floating. Also Frost found the use of shadow much more difficult, with none of the subtleties of Constable's shading, nor did he manage to give his sketch a true three-dimensional effect.

During the latter part of 1803 and throughout 1804, Constable continued to broaden his outlook, and improve his talents. He visited both Hampshire and Surrey, mainly to paint landscapes, although he also undertook several portrait commissions both on these visits and back home in Suffolk. He was also commissioned to paint an altarpiece for the Church of Saint Michael's in Brantham, one of three altarpieces he completed during his life. It must be stated that he was not successful in this particular aspect of art, maybe because he was not terribly interested in pseudo-religious subjects. I think it more likely that he was not capable of composing a picture in his own mind. He had to be able to sit down and paint what he saw in front of him, physical rather than imaginary.

This particular altarpiece represents Christ blessing the children — the child being held by Christ and blessed is thought to have been one of the daughters of John Lewis of Dedham, who later patronized Constable by commissioning portraits of his family.

Although the style bears some resemblance to that of Raphael, it is very poor by comparison, with very little depth of character.

At the end of October 1805, news reached England of the outcome of the Battle of Trafalgar — a glorious victory for the English Fleet off the Iberian coast, but the celebrations were marred by the death, in the hour of glory, of Lord Nelson. The entire nation was stunned by the loss of its most popular hero, and a feeling of shock and sadness hung gloomily over London. Constable, too, felt this sadness, and it prompted him to paint a watercolor, using his pencil sketches of 1803, when he had seen the «Victory» at anchor off Chatham, to depict the battle. It was a timely exhibit at the Royal Academy the following spring (1806), and received much attention and praise, although there were one or two unpleasant remarks about Constable trying to cash in on a moment of patriotism. Such remarks were totally unfounded, for Constable had felt sincerely sad over the loss of Nelson and the painting was his way of paying tribute to a great hero.

Ironically Turner also started a painting of the Battle of Trafalgar at the same time, and exhibited his version at his own gallery in the early part of 1806, despite the fact that it was unfinished. He did not complete the painting until 1808.

The year 1806 was Constable's most industrious so far, with a great number of paintings and drawings, including a self-portrait showing his still-youthful features. Several portrait commissions were also completed, including one for James Lloyd, the English poet and author, at whose home he met both Coleridge and Wordsworth. Lloyd was so pleased with his own portrait that he immediately asked Constable to paint the other members of his fairly large family, an endeavor which the never-rich painter eagerly accepted. Both portraits are in private family collections.

Lloyd's home was in Birmingham, which was where the portraits were painted, or at least begun, and although we have no definite date for the visit, it must have been in late August, for at the beginning of that month Constable had been at Epsom, and by September 1, he had embarked on a tour of the Lake District in northwest England.

That he was enchanted by the majesty of the lakeland scenery is beyond doubt; the lofty hills with their tumbling waterfalls provided an entirely new range of artistic viewpoints and aroused in him a new range of emotions. He was, however, unfortunate in not experiencing particularly clement weather, and many of his sketches, around seventy of which have so far been identified, bear the inscription «after rain,» «after storm,» and so forth. This preoccupation with the use of narrative in a title was a recurring theme with Constable. It stemmed in part from the tradition of the seventeenth and the eighteenth centuries, which was to include some narrative in the titles of paintings other than portraits. Although by Constable's time the tradition had largely died out, he continued to use it throughout his life, not merely because he was a traditionalist (far from it!) but because he was very aware of the nuances of light and shadow as the day progressed —— from the strong clear light of morning, high in the sky, through the lengthening shades of afternoon, to the low, mellow tones of evening, where the light is thrown upward from the horizon, creating deep shadows and silhouettes. Similarly with climatic conditions, he chose to include a narrative, primarily for his own use. In most of the sketches whose titles included a narrative, it was his intention to work up a full-size painting, using his notes to remind him of the exact conditions prevailing at the time he had perceived the scene. In the same way today, many painters use photographs to assist them, and to remind themselves of the varying tones.

Apart from his pencil sketches Constable also completed a number of watercolors, preferring this medium to the oils with which he was more accustomed. His preference for watercolor outside the studio is readily understood, for it was — and is — a much faster method of working and involved less equipment. Although today painters are fortunate in just being able to squeeze oil paint out of a tube, we must recall that around two hundred years ago, the pigment had to be ground and mixed on the spot, a craft in itself. Thus, apart from the quicker drying speed, watercolor was a far more practical medium for outdoor work.

At the time of his Lake District sojourn, Constable was still at an impressionable age, and, in his watercolors particularly, one can see the influence of Girtin.

Thomas Girtin was born in 1775, the same year as Turner, whose friend he was. Unlike Turner, Girtin favored the use of watercolor to oil, and was largely responsible for the revolutionary ideas connected with watercolor. After a visit to Paris in 1801 he began using rather absorbent off-white cartridge paper, and also swept away the idea of a monochrome underpainting, tending, instead, to wash in two or three colors of varying tone before he put in his firm painting.

His life was tragically cut short in 1802 at the age of twenty-six. Sir George Beaumont was an ardent admirer of his and greatly encouraged him, collecting several of his works and, for his own private enjoyment, copying them. Sir George showed some of Girtin's work to Constable prior to 1800, and advised him to be guided by the techniques pioneered by Girtin. Sir George also copied many of Girtin's Lake District paintings, and had shown these to Constable in the year before his visit to the Lakes. Probably, it was partly at Sir George's suggestion that Constable took himself off to the mountains, although the trip was paid for by his uncle, David Watts.

Constable found the scenery exciting, and was particularly thrilled by the ever-changing effects of light, as the fall storms raced across the mountaintops and through the valleys. Notwithstanding this, however, he was depressed in the desolate upland areas, and complained that he could find no churches or cottages with which to offset the bleak oppressiveness of the hills. Certainly his character was not of a type that can easily tolerate long periods of loneliness, and we cannot but admire his determination in remaining alone for so long in order to complete the work he had commenced. He had come to the lakes for the sole purpose of sketching, and he stuck to his ideas with a tenacity that was unusual for such a gentle, gregarious person.

His tour came to an end on, or around, October 19, at Langdale, after which he returned south to London, possibly stopping for a few days at the Lloyds' in Birmingham. His sketchbooks were full, he had completed several portraits, had broadened his style and technique considerably, and had sufficient material for paintings for the next few years.

As was to be expected, his submissions to the Royal Academy were nearly all of Lake District scenes, three of which, *View in Westmoreland, Keswick Lake,* * and *Bow Fell, Cumberland* were accepted and duly exhibited in the 1807 Exhibition. All are privately owned. Little else is known about Constable during this particular year, apart from the fact that he took up new lodgings at 13 Percy Street, and that he attended a dinner for Students of the Academy on November 16. He was also advised, by Thomas Stothard R. A., to seek election as an Associate of the Royal Academy; ironically, after a talk with Joseph Farington, a close friend and an academician, he felt it to be premature. He thus continued in London, throughout the year, completing several paintings from his sketches and understaking several portrait commissions, mainly for friends and family acquaintances. Portraits were, in those days, before the photograph, very much in vogue, and Constable completed well over a hundred in his career.

He also undertook what were known as house portraits for friends and acquaintances; this was a popular form of art at the time and gave employment to a great number of young artists. Constable painted his fair share, including views of Malvern Hall, Englefield House, Petworth House, Markfield House, and the previously mentioned East Bergholt House. While painting these stately homes must have been something of a chore to most artists, Constable does not seem to have found it too irritating, for he

---

* See p. 16.

19

Man-O-War, Chatham, 1803. Pencil, 8⅛″ × 16⅛″ (20.7 × 25.7 cm)
Victoria and Albert Museum, London

Shipping in the Thames, 1803
Pencil and greywash and watercolor, 7½" × 12⅜" (79.3 × 31.6 cm)
Victoria and Albert Museum, London

21

BOAT BUILDING NEAR FLATFORD MILL, 1815
Oil on canvas, 20″ × 24¼″ (50.8 × 61.6 cm)
Victoria and Albert Museum, London

23

Two Gleaners, c. 1815. Pencil, 3" × 3¾" (7.6 × 9.5 cm)
Musée du Louvre, Cabinet des Dessins, Paris

St. Mary-ad-Murum
Church, Colchester, seen
from the garden of a house
1813
Sketchbook page 5
Pencil, 3½" × 4¾"
(8.9 × 12 cm)
Victoria and Albert
Museum, London

Dedham Church, seen over a fence and
a clump of trees. 1813
Sketchbook page 65
Pencil, 3¹/₁₂" × 4³/₄" (8.9 × 12 cm)
Victoria and Albert Museum, London

THE MILL STREAM, 1814. Oil on canvas, 28″ × 36″ (71 × 91.5 cm)
Ipswich Art Gallery and Museum

FLATFORD MILL, 1817. Oil on canvas, 40″ × 50″ (102 × 127 cm)
The Tate Gallery, London

27

made several paintings of the ones we have mentioned. This repetitiveness seems to have been part of his character; although it was natural that he should paint many views of, for example, his beloved Suffolk, he did, in fact, paint the identical view on numerous occasions throughout his career, often returning to the exact spot after a gap of several years.

It is difficult to explain this satisfactorily. It has been suggested that he repainted a scene in order to satisfy himself and to gauge his development. While this is feasible, and very convenient for us, as we can observe his progress from year to year by reference to paintings of the same view, it does not entirely resolve the matter. Perhaps his self-consciousness restrained him from wandering too far off the beaten track, and he thus painted the same items over and over again; perhaps he was seeking perfection — not unknown in an artist, nor in a composer of music. Sibelius, for example, withdrew several of his works after they had been first performed in order to revise and improve them. It has been suggested, as well, that he repainted scenes that held for him a special emotional meaning; we know that he returned many times to the places where Maria Bicknell and he spent particularly happy moments together during their courtship, and, looking much further ahead, he returned, years later, after her death, to work on paintings of places that very definitely held strong sentimental memories.

We shall, of course, never know the truth; all that it is possible for us to do is to judge Constable's character from the tiny jigsaw pieces that a study of his life affords us.

His submissions to the Academy over the next few years were primarily of Lake District scenes, five of which were shown in 1808 and a further three in 1809; in the latter year also, he showed five Lake District scenes in the British Institution Exhibition.

In August he was at Malvern Hall, in Warwickshire, undertaking portraits for which he had been commissioned, and, while there, made several paintings of the house itself and the very spacious grounds.

He returned to East Bergholt sometime in early September, just as the last of the harvest was being brought in from the fields and as the leaves began to turn their fascinating colors of gold and russet brown.

It was during this fall visit that he met and immediately fell in love with Maria Bicknell, an attractive, dark-haired, twenty-one-year-old girl whom he had known informally since the turn of the century.

TURMOIL — 1809–1816

Maria was the oldest daughter of Charles Bicknell and his second wife, the daughter of the rector of East Bergholt, Dr. Rhudde. Charles Bicknell was a man of good standing and had carved out for himself a career in the Civil Service, rising to become a secretary to the Prince of Wales (later to become King of England) before moving on to be Solicitor to the Admiralty, a highly respected position. His second father-in-law, Dr. Rhudde, had also served at Court, as one of the chaplains to the Prince of Wales.

Maria was born on January 15, 1788, but, like many of her family, suffered from tuberculosis and was thus a weak and frail child. The family lived in London, primarily because of her father's commitments, but because of her ill-health, Maria spent much of her youth at East Bergholt with her maternal grandfather. Exactly when she met John is uncertain, but we do know that they fell in love in late 1809, and, although they were to be apart for long periods, they wrote often to each other.

Their courtship was to be a protracted affair, with many upsets which had their effect on Constable, and thus on his paintings. He became a slave to his emotions, acting, sometimes, almost desperately, as, for example when, in 1811, on receiving a letter from Maria advising him to forget her as the obstacles to their marriage were insurmountable, he jumped on the first available coach and dashed halfway across the country to persuade her that all was not lost. While this sort of behavior would be understandable in a youth infatuated with a first love, it must be remembered that at this time Constable was thirty-five years old.

It was unfortunate that the years 1810 to 1816 were so full of emotional stress for Constable for he had, by 1810, virtually completed a self-imposed apprenticeship and was now equipped to undertake the paintings for which he has become famous. He was striving for perfection in an unusual area of painting — pure landscape.

Until the middle of the sixteenth century paintings had been of a religious nature (apart from portraits), with only a small amount of landscape as a background to the main theme. Much of the landscape in background was only symbolic and did not reflect any real view. The first landscapists who could be called worthy of the title were the seventeenth-century Dutch artists such as Ruisdael and

Self-Portrait, 1806. Drawing, 9⅛″ × 5¾″ (23.2 × 14.7 cm). Private collection

Vermeer; the style was then taken up by the French and Venetian painters, the most famous of whom was probably Canaletto, and then reached England by the time of Gainsborough. Although Gainsborough painted primarily portraits, he did introduce landscapes into his background, and, unlike the earlier religious or Court painters of Europe, his landscapes were realistic.

Turner refined the art, though many of his works were of a misty, impressionistic style, but it was Constable who decided to paint «pure» landscapes — a very bold step for a young, unknown painter.

Although he was self-conscious and unsure of his talent, if not his direction, he knew that for him there was only one style to pursue. All he needed was the moral encouragement and the right emotional frame of mind to undertake it, and while his parents did their best to give him this encouragement and security, his turbulent love affair was an unsettling factor that probably delayed the moment when his genius was fully comprehensible.

It was doubly regrettable that the opposition to their proposed marriage, once Maria and John had made their respective parents aware of their intentions, was not from any of the parents, but from the old and embittered Dr. Rhudde, Maria's grandfather. Nor was this opposition, which was at times virulent, directed at John, but against his father, Golding. It was one of the tragic consequences of petty village politics, but Rhudde's determination to prevent the marriage was, for a long time, most effective.

The emotional stress of this period had a serious effect on Constable's health, forcing him to spend many weeks at the East Bergholt home in order to convalesce. Maria also suffered as a result of the forced separation from the man she loved, but she maintained that strict self-control and decorum that has nowadays all but disappeared from our way of life. She wrote to John on November 2, 1811: «I shall be guided by my father in every respect. Should he acquiesce in my wishes I shall be happier than I can express.» But it was to no avail. Dr. Rhudde's determination to keep the young couple apart grew into an obsession; he went so far as to disown his granddaughter when he found out that she had been secretly seeing Constable.

But Rhudde's determination to stop their courtship was met only by Constable's doggedness in continuing it. Maria, helplessly caught in the middle, and frustrated by the obstinacy of her grandfather, and by now her father as well, broke off their engagement, believing their chances of being given permission to marry to be so slight as to be nonexistent. She begged John not to torture himself with hopeless optimism any longer. But his heart was set, and he resolved to continue pressing his affections for as long as was necessary to wear down the opposition.

Throughout all the stresses of this affair he had to keep painting — and this was probably the savior of his sanity, for he found, in his work, the outlet for his pent-up emotions.

In September of 1811 he visited Salisbury at the invitation of his old friend Fisher, now bishop of that diocese, and spent several weeks sketching in and around the ancient city. He fell in love with Salisbury and its graceful cathedral, set in meadows to the south of the city, its lofty spire leaping skyward above the green pastures. On this visit too, he first met the bishop's nephew, also called John Fisher. The two of them became firm friends and remained so until the death of Fisher many years later.*

Several sketches of the cathedral, made on that visit, survive, and a number of paintings were derived from them, including the view of Salisbury now hanging in the Louvre, Paris. This was Constable's major exhibit at the 1812 Academy exhibition. As with many of his favorite locations, Constable was to return to Salisbury for inspiration many times in the future. Yet another spot to which he returned and painted many times was Flatford Mill, back home in East Anglia. One of the many versions of this was exhibited alongside the *Salisbury.*

Many of these early paintings — probably up to about 1817 — often have the appearance of having been done in great haste without the degree of care or concern with detail for which Constable was later to be known. The years 1808 to 1812 in particular seem to indicate a bad patch, with the majority of the paintings of this period looking as if they are intended as no more than sketches. Constable was later chided for his lack of «finish,» a point to which we shall return, but two paintings of this time, chosen at random, are worth examining, if for no other reason than to be aware of the improvement over the following years.

The first is *A Lane Near East Bergholt,*** painted on October 13, 1809. It is fairly small and was painted on board — on the back of the board is an unidentified country house. The painting itself is really no more than a sketch, showing a man resting against a milestone in the late-

---

* See p. 44.   ** See p. 34.

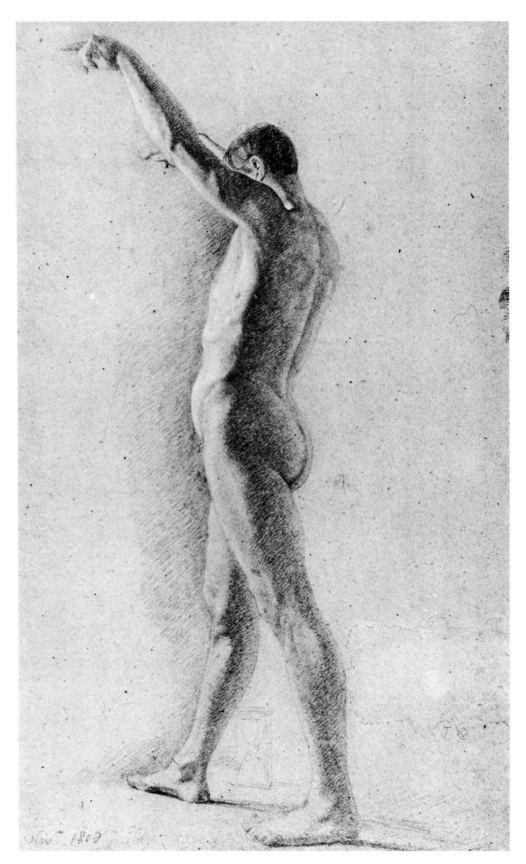

Life Study, 1808
Drawing, 21″ × 12½″
(53.3 × 31.8 cm)
Colchester and Essex
Museum, England

31

afternoon sun. The form of the man is very hazy — almost impressionistic — with no clearly defined features to his face. This in itself was nothing new in art, being a device used by many painters when they wished to indicate a person without using too much detail. In this instance Constable does not seem to have made the man significant enough — being in the center of the picture he automatically attracts attention, yet the eye is drawn away to the two trees on the right, the true focal point. He did suffer with his foregrounds, never being able to overcome the problem of a lead-in. Had he put the man to the left of the picture he might have overcome it here.

Unlike his later paintings the trees here are lacking in detail, having been blocked in hastily; they are, thus, lacking in three-dimensional quality. The shadows they cast, too, do not seem very clear.

Lest it be said that the picture has no good points, the left foreground, rich, warm dark colors, and the hills in the background, which convey exactly the impression of distance, do show that Constable had talent, but of course it needed refining. The other painting, of the same period, was a view that Constable painted many times — at least six paintings survive; *Flatford Mill from the Lock* was an ideal place to sit and sketch — calm, peaceful, and close to home. In 1810 alone he painted it three times, ignoring pencil sketches. His uncle, David Pike Watts, had seen one of these sketches on Constable's easel and had taken an immediate fancy to it, telling the painter that he would like it when finished, for its detail rather than its overall effect. Looking at the three sketches of that year, this statement seems rather strange, for none of them is particularly overflowing in intricate detail.

The painting we are examining here, which is privately owned, has, again, the blocked-in trees without much character. The mill itself does exude some character, though not much in the way of detail, but this is rather dissolved by the appalling manner in which the sky has been put in *after* the main work. The heavy brushstrokes of the cloud stand out glaringly, distracting the eye.

The quality of the picture lies in the stream and its sense of depth and reflective power, though the big splash of white does detract a little. The gentle touches of white in the middle of the stream (a device used to indicate the glint of light reflecting off the water) are good, probably having been delicately touched on with a knife, but this big blob of white that overflows onto the bank has been brushed on. Looking at some of these early sketches, it is not difficult to understand why Constable was not, at that time, particularly revered as a great landscapist. He did, happily, improve.

During this period his health was not at its best, though how much this was due to emotional problems we can never be sure. In the summer of 1812, having shown his landscape of Salisbury at the Academy, he returned to Suffolk, and was, for a time, so ill that he could not summon the strength to paint. There had been a slight disagreement with Maria, which was probably one of the causes of his illness, though in reality this was probably the straw that broke the camel's back. But by late August Maria was again writing to « my dearest John, » and she seemed to have dispelled some of her earlier pessimism, having noticed an apparent thawing in her father's opposition to a wedding. The thaw was not to last, however, for by the end of the year Mr. Bicknell had again reiterated his adamant refusal to countenance his daughter's union with this « upstart country artist — the son of a village miller. » By January 1813, poor Constable had even been refused entry to the Bicknell household, being turned away from the door when he called to inquire after Maria's health that winter.

Mrs. Constable intervened on behalf of her son, and called on Mr. Bicknell in April in an effort to gain permission for John to visit Maria. But this, too, was to no avail. John left London for Suffolk in late May. The summer turned out to be one of the hottest in living memory, and, unable to see any progress along the path to matrimony, he threw himself into his work, aware that if once he sat and thought about his predicament, he would become more depressed and would simply mope about listlessly.

The sketchbook he filled that summer, with its hot, sunny days and large harvest, is a remarkable record of his tenacity and of his talent, for he worked almost every day, completing 132 pencil sketches in fifteen hectic weeks. The subjects cover a remarkable range, from tombstones in a village churchyard to the gathering of the harvest; flower studies, sheep and cattle in the fields, mooring posts by the river; the mills and locks on the river itself; and a number of views that he referred to in later years for some of his great paintings, such as *The White Horse,* * *The Leaping Horse,* ** *The Valley Farm* *** and *Stratford Mill.* He also painted a major picture for the following year's Academy, *Ploughing Scene in Suffolk.* This painting was to have a checkered future, for it was changed, first by another artist, who altered the

---

* See front cover.   ** See p. 59.   *** See p. 85.

CART AND HORSES, October 1814. Oil on paper, 6½″ × 9⅜″ (16.5 × 23.8 cm)
Victoria and Albert Museum, London

Lane Near East Bergholt, 1809. Oil on canvas, 8½″ × 12⅞″ (21.6 × 32.7 cm)
Collection: Thos. Agnew and Sons, London

BARGES ON THE STOUR, 1810. Oil on paper laid on canvas, 10¼″ × 12¼″ (26 × 31.1 cm)
Victoria and Albert Museum, London

AUTUMNAL SUNSET, c. 1812. Oil on paper and canvas, 6¾″ × 13¼″ (17.1 × 33.6 cm)
Victoria and Albert Museum, London

36

WEYMOUTH BAY, 1816. Oil on canvas, 22″ × 30¼″ (56 × 77 cm)
Museum of Fine Arts, Boston. Bequest of Mr. and Mrs. Caleb Lormy

STUDY FOR THE HAY-WAIN, c. 1821. Oil on canvas, 54″ × 74″ (137 × 188 cm)
Victoria and Albert Museum, London

THE HAY-WAIN, 1821. Oil on canvas, $51\frac{1}{4}'' \times 73''$ (130 × 185.5 cm)
The National Gallery, London

MARIA WITH TWO CHILDREN, 1820. Oil on wood, 6⅛″ × 8¾″ (15.5 × 22.2 cm)
Private collection

▷
MARIA BICKNELL, 1816. Oil on canvas, 11⅞″ × 9⅞″ (30.2 × 25.2 cm)
The Tate Gallery, London

41

ANN CONSTABLE, date unknown. Oil on canvas, 30″ × 25″ (76 × 63.5 cm). Private collection

GOLDING CONSTABLE, c. 1815. Oil on canvas, 29¾″ × 24¾″ (75.5 × 63 cm). Private collection

Archdeacon John Fisher, 1817. Oil on canvas, 14⅛″ × 12″ (36 × 30.5 cm)
Fitzwilliam Museum, Cambridge

sky, then by Constable himself, when he put back his original sky, and slightly reduced the size. He also painted another version of it.

Two sketches of this period are also worth noting for their insight into his development, for they show particularly his increased understanding of the effects of light, his better representation of cloud, and his persistent difficulty in portraying foregrounds effectively.

The first of the two, *Autumnal Sunset* * is a delightfully warm study, peaceful and calm, the farmhands preparing to hurry away home after a full day in the fields, and the rooks hastening to their nests as the sun dips behind the distant hills. This picture is perfectly balanced — the warm glow of the sun contrasting well with the dark shadows of the hills in the center of the painting. The other sketch, again in oil, is also very pleasing, aesthetically, with its distant glimmer of the sea, probably near Harwich, and the high billowing clouds, leading the eye into the scene. The sky in this sketch is particularly pleasing, and shows a great deal of care, understanding, and talent, the more so as it seems certain that this was painted on the spot and not in the studio. That Constable was having difficulty with his foregrounds is obvious, for the corn is not very well defined, and there is no threshold over which the viewer can step into the picture.

The summer of 1814 was again hot and sunny, and again Constable threw himself into his work, completing another remarkable sketchbook, as well as several major paintings. The most important of these, and one which Constable claimed to have painted entirely in the open air, was *Boat Building on the Stour*. He had made a sketch, in pencil, of this scene on September 7, 1814, and must have returned to paint it fairly soon thereafter. The boatyard was owned by his father — only a short distance frrom Flatford Mill — and John worked there each afternoon until the painting was nearly complete, leaving only a few minor details to be added in the studio that winter. He worked for a set time each afternoon, knowing when it was time to stop for the day by the encroaching shadows and by the smoke from a distant cottage chimney, announcing that the fire had been lit to cook the laborers' supper on their return from the fields.

He was working concurrently, in the mornings it would seem, on another «outdoor» painting, the *View of Dedham*, which had been commissioned by a family friend, Thomas Fitzhugh, on the occasion of his marriage to Miss Philadelphia Godfrey (whose father owned East Bergholt House, a painting of which was Constable's earliest commission in 1801). Their marriage took place on November 11, and the painting was complete by then. It is now in the Leeds Art Gallery. Both of the above pictures, along with six others, were shown at the 1815 Academy, but before the opening of the Exhibition, tragedy had struck.

Sunday, April 9, was warm and sunny, a pleasant spring day; Ann Constable, the painter's mother, having been to church that morning and received Communion from the hands of Dr. Rhudde, whose opposition to her son's marriage would not deter her from her Christian duties, was doing some gardening. In midafternoon, she suffered a stroke and had to be carried to her bed, partially paralyzed. A month later, on May 8, she died.

Her son was deeply grieved, for not only had he lost a mother but also a dear friend who had consistently encouraged him in spite of her own fears about his wisdom in choosing such a precarious profession, and it was she who had inspired him in his amatory ambitions.

John was too deeply grieved to attend his mother's funeral, a fact which was to have a strange sequel many years later. He called on Maria in London on May 12 to inform her of his loss. He was greeted with sympathy and understanding, but also with the news that Maria's mother had died the previous day, after a long illness. Thus it was that the two lovers shared the common grief of mourning.

The specter of death was to appear again that summer with the news that John's favorite cousin, James Gubbins, had been killed in action at the Battle of Waterloo that June.

One year and six days after his wife's death, Golding Constable followed her to the grave — he had never recovered his strength after the shock of her death. The family business was entrusted, in Golding's will, to Abram, to manage on behalf of the other members of the family. John was thus assured an income of four hundred pounds per annum, quite a reasonable sum in the early nineteenth century.

Certain of this regular income to supplement his earnings from painting, John felt slightly reassured and decided to press Maria to marry him. Dr. Rhudde was now eighty-two, and his opposition, although still as strong, was not so effective, and Mr. Bicknell was still distressed by his wife's decease. Maria was torn between her growing love for John, and the fear of her father's inevitable wrath, but finally she decided, and in a quiet ceremony in St. Martins-in-the-Fields, London (in what is now Trafalgar Square), conducted by John Fisher, John Constable married Maria Bicknell. No member of either family was present.

---

* See p. 36.

A NEW BEGINNING — 1816–1820

The couple left for a honeymoon at the Dorset vicarage of John Fisher (who had himself only been married a couple of months) in the village of Osmington, near Weymouth.

During the honeymoon, Constable went down into Weymouth Bay, where he painted his sketch of the same name.* It is a fine picture, in which we can see the billowing storm clouds being chased into giant patterns by the early winter winds and the stormy seas being hurled up on the beach. The spot is quite remote, and even today, it is possible to savor the same experience of gale-tossed seas that so excited Constable.

At last, his dream had come true — Maria was his wife. He had, of course, lost both parents, but his life as an adult now stood before him, with all its responsibilities. Now, he *must* paint.

A sense of relief swept over Constable once the marriage was complete, after such a long wait, and he now felt confident enough to immerse himself totally in painting. He had, it is true, additional financial responsibilities, but these were outweighed by the sheer joy of living with someone as placid and kind as Maria. Returning from their honeymoon on December 9, Maria discovered she was pregnant, which must have given Constable immense joy, but also jolted him into looking for a house suitable to accommodate a family. Unfortunately Maria suffered a miscarriage the next February, but became pregnant again almost immediately. Constable was, at the time, working on his *Flatford Mill*** painting for the Royal Academy. This was the forerunner to the series of six-foot canvases he was to show in the years following — this one being 102 by 127 cms, and he had been working on it before his marriage, taking the scene directly from his 1814 sketchbook. He had not had time to complete it before his marriage, and it was only at the urging of Joseph Farington that he proceeded with it in February in order to submit it for the exhibition. For the first time, bargehorses and human figures form the central theme, bringing a new dimension into his paintings; it also appears to be finished — we must recall that many of Constable's critics had earlier complained that his pictures looked unfinished.

Despite the compliments the painting received when it was shown at the Academy, it failed to sell, and was thus returned to its painter, who set about making alterations, particularly to the trees on the right. (It is possible, from X-rays, to detect the earlier outline of these.) It was not unusual for Constable to alter his paintings after they had been exhibited, or even after they had been sold, much to the later consternation of John Fisher, for we must remember that he wanted perfection, and, as any painter knows, it is very tempting to slightly change a picture some time after its completion.

Before leaving London for the summer in Suffolk, Constable managed to find the house he wanted, at No 1 Keppel Street, close to Russell Square, which, although now an integral part of London, was then on the northern boundary of the metropolis with green fields and farmland beyond. Constable took a seven-year lease on the house and spent several weeks preparing it for occupation while Maria stayed at her father's house on Putney Common, then a country village but now, like Russell Square, part of London. There had been a slight reconciliation with Mr. Bicknell who, faced with a fait accompli, and mellowed by age, accepted the situation with grace if not with enthusiasm.

The summer and early fall passed happily at East Bergholt, with John busily sketching in preparation for a winter's painting and Maria being fussed over by relatives and friends. The annual routine had now been firmly established, of sketching in the open air throughout the summer while the weather was good, and then completing the paintings in the studio through the dark, cold months of winter, a routine followed by many of today's painters. Portraits were also completed, preferably during the winter, although this was not always possible as the person commissioning such a work normally dictated the times of the sittings. This portraiture still provided the main part of Constable's income, though with the amount he received from the family business, he was to feel reasonably secure financially.

Although we have no definite identification of the oil studies he completed that summer, they were well spoken of by friends who saw them, and it seems reasonable to assume, therefore, that he was at peace with the world, as should be expected after his marriage to Maria, the importance of which must not be underestimated.

On December 4, Maria gave birth to a son, who was named John Charles, after his father and maternal grandfather.

---

* See p. 37.   ** See p. 27.

Much of the following year (1818) was taken up in attending to several matters relating to the sale of the old family house at East Bergholt, which must have caused Constable and his brothers and sisters some distress, as they prepared to sell all the items that had been so familiar to them as they grew up. The sale was arranged that November, but was not finalized until May 1819. By a strange irony, Constable arrived in East Bergholt on the sixth of that month to be greeted by the tolling of the church bell heralding the death, that morning, of Dr. Rhudde. Rhudde had, for so long, obstructed Maria's marriage, and had even disowned her, but on his deathbed had changed his will, leaving her the beneficiary of the princely sum of four thousand pounds. Added to the proceeds from the sale of the house, this now meant that the growing family of the painter was at last released from any lingering financial worries.

Prior to his visit to East Bergholt, Constable had submitted his most ambitious picture thus far to the Academy — the first of his six-foot canvases.

The *Scene on the River Stour** shows a large grayish-white horse being ferried across the river from one bank to the other, a common enough feature of the time as the towpath occasionally changed sides to avoid some obstruction on the bank. The horse, which would normally have been pulling the barge, became, temporarily, the passenger, and having been coaxed into the vessel was ferried across, either by helpers on the far bank pulling on ropes, or the barge hands poling the barge across, as in this picture. The scene is one Constable would have watched countless times during his boyhood, and the section of river on which this picture was painted was very close to the family business premises.

Farington had urged Constable to pay greater attention to the finish of his paintings, a suggestion that had also been made by Constable's father some time earlier. It seems that the painter was sometimes too anxious to complete a grand scene, too impatient to pay that extra attention to the final brushstrokes, and his paintings suffered as a result. When we look closely at some of his paintings we can see this lack of finish. There are short, rough strokes, sometimes almost blotches of paint that look as though they had been put onto the canvas but not painted in. It is tempting to say that Constable was a careless painter, but this is very far from the truth, for he paid the most intricate attention to detail. Apart from some of his very late paintings, which suggest the work of an old and tired man, his canvases are full of life and exact, minute detail. He was a painter of nature, and he understood his subject completely, down to the fauna of an area at a particular time of year; his portrayal of trees in some of his paintings are almost a natural history lesson in themselves. Yet still his paintings seemed unfinished, almost as if he had not quite had time to complete them before rushing them off to an exhibition. And that is exactly what happened. He was impatient, we know, not with people, but with the need to finish a scene. He was aware that if he spent too much time on detail in one picture he would never finish it nor have time to paint any others. (This is one reason he later stopped painting six-foot canvases.) It was what we would today describe as the pressures of business, the financial necessity to complete and sell a painting.

So why then did he decide to paint a very large canvas, which would take so much more time to complete?

Constable's first major attempt at an extra large picture had been in 1817 when he painted *Flatford Mill* which received a great deal of favorable comment even though it did not sell. In it Constable had attempted to introduce more detail of a technical nature, and he took this a step further in the cold winter of 1818–1819 when he began work on the painting that became known as *The White Horse.** In this, his first six-foot canvas, he tried to introduce more of nature's delicate detail. In smaller pictures, much of this detail was lost, and it was Constable's intention to show his public that this beauty existed.

But this was not the only reason. Constable needed and wanted attention — not necessarily praise, though this was obviously welcome — nor was he seeking extra financial reward for a larger canvas. He must have been aware that any canvas of this size would automatically attract attention, but just as in 1805 when he had completed his tribute to Nelson and the victors of Trafalgar, this was not a cold and calculated attempt to attract attention.

Spurred on by the laudatory success of *Flatford Mill*, he drove himself to even greater heights, setting himself a challenge that he eagerly accepted. He knew he was capable of producing a picture that could stand up to attention, and for a man as shy and self-conscious as Constable, this was indeed an achievement.

His marriage had at long last given him a degree of stability and Maria's gentle and placid companionship offered him sufficient courage to attempt such a task, particularly when it is remembered that landscape painting was still not a respected art.

_____

* See front cover.

His gamble paid off. The picture, when it was hung at the Royal Academy exhibition in the spring of 1819, received much attention and prompted much discussion, the overwhelming majority of it favorable. Among its most ardent admirers was John Fisher, who had come to the exhibition from Salisbury. It was he who gave it its famous name, for Constable had exhibited it under the title of *Scene on the River Stour.*

Fisher asked Constable to sell him the painting. There was a delay in the transaction while a price was discussed, but by July 20, a letter had arrived for Constable with a firm offer of one hundred guineas. The amount was more than double anything Constable had ever received for one picture, and he was thus overjoyed. The day before this letter had arrived, his wife Maria had given birth to their second child, Maria Louisa (who was to be known as Minna). The tide of fortune seemed, at last, to have turned in his favor. His wife and two children were well, his work was being appreciated, and his immediate financial anxieties were over.

To end the year in fine style he gained Associate membership of the Academy, beating C. R. Leslie (later his close friend and first biographer) in the November elections by eight votes to five.

For much of that winter he was working on the second of his large canvases, *Stratford Mill* which was, after his death, to become known as *The Young Waltonians* * for reasons that have been surmised but never proven. The picture has remained a firm favorite with Constable admirers, due partly to its rustic qualities and gentle features. It shows the river Stour, looking upstream toward the mill at Stratford Saint Mary.

The Young Waltonians shows a far greater insight into the art of large landscape painting than the previous effort. It does not contain quite so much fine detail, thus leading the eye into the picture with none of the distractions of sharply defined objects. Constable was, justifiably, very proud of this painting and went to great lengths to explain the picture to some of his friends. He emphasized that one must understand what one was painting in order to portray nature correctly, and went on to explain that « when water reaches the roots of plants or trees the action on the extremities of their roots is such they no longer vegetate but die, which explains the appearance of the dead tree on the edge of the stream. » He also pointed out that the action of the wind blowing across the meadows onto the boles of the trees inclines them to the left of the picture. Constable was to come in for some criticism, from the man who acquired the picture, John Tinney, a solicitor who acted for Fisher and was given the painting as a gift after winning a lawsuit, for the skies, which he found « too prominent. » This prompted Constable to pronounce firmly that « the landscape painter who does not make his skies a very material part of his composition neglects to avail himself of one of his greatest aids — it will be difficult to name a class of Landscape in which the sky is not the "key note" . . . and the "organ of sentiment". »

Looking at the painting today, it is difficult to envisage why Tinney should have made this criticism, for the sky, far from being too prominent, blends gently into the overall tranquillity of the picture.

Once the 1820 Exhibition was over, Constable took his family to stay with the bishop at Salisbury. The visit gave him an opportunity to make several sketches in Wiltshire and the New Forest before returning to London in late August. The capital was in uproar and Constable immediately took the family to the relative safety of Hampstead, where, the previous summer, they had rented a cottage for a few months. The disturbances in London surrounded the return to England of Queen Caroline, the harlot wife of George IV, who had succeeded to the throne on the death of his father on January 29. Caroline had left her husband when he was Prince Regent to live with another man, who, in his turn, had been followed by a motley procession of lovers, both in England and in Europe, to where Caroline had been banished by the English Court. She returned to claim the title of Queen, as the marriage had not been dissolved, and this led to the rousing of passions as the two sides pushed the relative merits of their case. There had been attempts on the lives of several Cabinet ministers, and it was not until the late summer that peace was restored. Even then, it took the spectacle of many public hangings to quieten things down.

On November 21 Farington called on Constable, now back in the capital, and saw him working on a picture depicting the opening of Waterloo Bridge (June 18, 1817), which the painter had attended and sketched, with the intention of making a painting. On being asked his opinion, Farington said that he thought Constable would do better to produce a landscape similar to his last great one, *The Young Waltonians,* whereupon Constable put aside his Waterloo (subsequently not to be completed until 1832) and set to work on the painting for which, more than any other work, we remember him.

---

* Now in a private collection.

The Hay-Wain. In later years he was also used extensively to replicate several of Constable's smaller pictures, mainly those for which a definite sale was forthcoming.

The Hay-Wain is so well known that no description of it is necessary. The colors are clear and natural, yet blend gracefully into one another; the lighting is as perfect as that supplied by Nature herself; the size and magnificence of the entire painting are breathtaking.

Incredibly the public at the 1821 Academy did not think so, for it failed to sell and had to be taken back to Constable's studio. It only aroused the interest of the art world in 1824 when it was shown at the Paris Salon and bought by a Paris dealer, John Arrowsmith, to whom we shall return later.

Shortly before the Exhibition opened, Maria gave birth to their third child, Charles Golding.

In June, Constable accompanied John Fisher, now ordained as an archdeacon, on his visit to Berkshire, making many sketches of the countryside around Reading, Newbury, Oxford, and Blenheim Palace, the birthplace of Winston Churchill. It was evident, on his return to the capital in July, that his family reeded to escape from the noise and grime of the city. They went to Hampstead, where they rented a house in Lower Terrace, from where one had a fine view of the city laid out below, from Westminster to Greenwich. It was here, for the first time, that Constable began his serious studies of the effects of skies. He had, of course, always been interested in the effects of light and cloud, and we can recall his enthusiasm for the giant storm clouds he encountered on his «Coutts» voyage some eighteen years earlier, but it was here, at Hampstead in 1821, that he turned to a genuine study of cloud patterns and produced many sketches, both oil and water, of skies.*

He visited Suffolk in September to undertake his third religious commission, an altarpiece for the church at Manningtree, which brought him two hundred pounds.

By early November the family had returned to London, and Constable went off to Salisbury to stay with the bishop. He did not return to London until shortly before Christmas, which was clouded that year by the death of Joseph Farington, his constant friend and adviser since he first came to London in 1799. The following February he took Maria to look over Farington's old house at 35 Charlotte Street, and they moved into it in November.

In the meantime, while he was busily retouching the five pictures he was to show at the 1822 Academy, he was approached by Arrowsmith with an offer to buy the *Hay-Wain* for seventy pounds. Although Constable was in need of money at the time — for the improvements to Farington's old house were costly — he refused to let the picture go for this trifling amount, knowing in his own mind that it was worth far more.

Apart from being quite costly, the move to Charlotte Street was very harrowing and caused Constable much distress through their first winter there. While the carpenters, bricklayers, and decorators were working in the house prior to the arrival of the family (who were, together with the newest member, Isabel, born on August 23, still living in Hampstead), Constable was trying very hard to be in three places at once — at Hampstead with the family, at Charlotte Street, where the mess annoyed him, and in Suffolk, where he was working on the Manningtree altarpiece. His health, inevitably, suffered. The winter was cold and damp, Maria was ill, laid low by an attack of pneumonia, which caused her husband much anxiety. She was never strong, and the strain of five pregnancies in six years had not helped; and to cap it all, John Charles, the oldest son, was also sick.

This was probably the first winter that Constable suffered from rheumatism, which was to afflict him so much in later years and severely curtail his painting, but through most of the winter of 1822–1823 he managed to keep on working, though often in pain. By Christmas he had dispatched the Manningtree altarpiece, and had started work on two six-footers, one of which, *Salisbury Cathedral from the Bishop's Grounds*, was exhibited at the 1823 Academy.**

In his earlier days Constable had made a fair living from house portraits. We will remember that his first commissioned work was a painting of East Bergholt House. Despite this, he had never enjoyed painting in the fine architectural detail of the type found in a cathedral, so it was somewhat surprising that he chose this as the subject for a major painting. Bishop Fisher had commissioned a painting of his favorite building, so it was partly out of deference to the good bishop that the artist made his decision. Constable had sketched the cathedral many times, to the bishop's delight, and it was from several of these sketches that Constable took his inspiration for the major picture.

Constable labored all winter on the canvas and was quite pleased with the outcome, even though he compained to the bishop several times about his lack of conviction when painting the intricacies of a

---

* See pp. 49–52.   ** See p. 57.

STUDY FOR CUMULUS CLOUDS, 1822. Oil on canvas, 12″ × 20″ (30,5 × 51 cm)
Yale Center for British Art, New Haven, Conn. Paul Mellon Collection

human architect (interestingly, he did not object to the detail of Nature!), such as the numerous windows and buttresses. There was also a disagreement over the sky. The bishop was rather put out to find that Constable had put a large cloud on the canvas, with dashes of blue sky to offset the verdant foreground. The bishop wanted to see the sky free of any occlusion, with bright celestial light shining down on his magnificent building. Several letters passed, but both parties stuck firmly to their point of view, yet without any hostility, and the bishop bore no malice when the painting appeared at the 1823 Academy — with clouds!

We have, in this small episode, a further confirmation of Constable's determination, once he had made up his mind on a subject. With all the problems he had that winter, it would have been quite simple for him to have quietly acceded to the bishop's wishes, but he chose to make his point that when it came to painting, he knew best.

However, the matter did not rest there, for in July 1824 the canvas was returned to its author ostensibly for renovation but in reality for the removal of the clouds. Constable compromised. He made a new version, without clouds. While the original now hangs in the Victoria & Albert Museum in London, the second version, completed in 1826, can now be seen in the Frick Collection in New York City. The bishop died before it was completed. Both paintings are magnificent, giving a perfect reflection of the serenity and calm surrounding an English cathedral. Happily — apart from the distant drone of traffic — this calm persists today particularly on a warm summer's afternoon, and Salisbury retains its charm as one of England's loveliest cathedrals, exactly as Constable portrayed it.

Having placed the *Cathedral* in the Academy, Constable spent some weeks with his family in London before leaving for a visit to the Fishers in August. He stayed with them for six weeks, proof if it is needed that there was no hostility between them.

A brief return to London preceded a journey north to Coleorton Hall, Sir George Beaumont's country home, near Ashby-de-la-Zouche in Leicestershire.

It is uncertain just how much financial help Sir George gave to Constable, particularly in his early days, but there can be no doubting the influence he had on the painter's career, both by his friendship and encouragement and through introductions to friends.

The visit to Coleorton was extended, and was only brought to a conclusion by the increasingly persistent pleadings of Maria for his return to the family in London. It was not that Constable was glad to be away from the children and his wife — all of whom he loved very much — it was, rather, that he became so deeply involved in copying many of the paintings in Sir George's collection, among which were more Claudes, that he forgot time completely. He found new aspects in art, fresh inspiration, and new heights to aim for. His painting had reached a stage where he needed, if not a fresh direction, new encouragement. His work was selling reasonably enough, though not as well as some of the more popular painters, such as Turner, but he was always adamant that he would not paint to satisfy a fickle public, but would continue to portray Nature as she was.

Although this declaration, which he made to Fisher, was partly a jibe at Turner, whose work was becoming more and more «airy,» full of misty visions and translucence, Constable did firmly hold the belief that his «pure» landscapes were the only way for him.

The major picture he exhibited at the Academy in 1824 was *A Boat Passing a Lock,** a further magnificent view of Suffolk, though not, this time, a six-footer, probably because he did not have the time. This, again, was a view he had painted before and was to paint again. Arrowsmith had returned from Paris shortly before the Exhibition began, and this time a deal was consummated, with Constable selling *The Hay-Wain* and two other pictures in return for two hundred and fifty pounds, a mutually agreeable price, particularly as there had been no other interest in Constable's most popular (nowadays) painting. The Academy painting that year was sold on the first day for one hundred and fifty pounds.

Maria's health was, at this time, causing extra concern, and in an attempt to clear her lungs of the winter's smoke from London chimneys, Constable took her and the children to Brighton. The seaside resort was then at the height of its popularity, being patronized by the king and thus the society of the day. Constable hated it, from the first moment he set foot in it: «Piccadilly, or worse, by the seaside!» he wrote off angrily to Fisher. He found good lodgings for Maria and the children and raced back to London to get on with his painting. The day before his letter to Fisher, the Salon had opened in Paris, and gold medals were awarded by Charles X to two pictures: Delacroix's *Massacre at Chios* and *The Hay-Wain.*

---

* See p. 60.

Elm Trees in Old Hall Park, East Bergholt, October 22, 1817
Pencil, with grey and white washes, 23¼″ × 19½″ (59.2 × 49.4 cm)
Victoria and Albert Museum, London
◁

Overbury Hall, August 20, 1815.   Pencil, 4½″ × 7⅛″ (11.5 × 18 1 cm)
Victoria and Albert Museum, London

Salisbury Cathedral W. Door, August 22, 1820
Pencil, 4½" × 7¼" (11.5 × 18.5 cm). Victoria and Albert Museum, London

SALISBURY CATHEDRAL FROM THE BISHOP'S GROUNDS, 1823
Oil on canvas, 34½″ × 44″ (87.6 × 111.8 cm). Victoria and Albert Museum, London

STUDY FOR THE LEAPING HORSE, c. 1825. Oil on canvas, 51″ × 74″ (129.4 × 188 cm)
Victoria and Albert Museum, London

THE LEAPING HORSE, 1825. Oil on canvas, 66″ × 73¾″ (167.5 × 187 cm)
The Royal Academy of Arts, London

BOAT PASSING A LOCK, 1824. Oil on canvas, 56″ × 47½″ (142 × 120.5 cm)
Walter Morrison Picture Settlement. On view at Sudeley Castle, England

Thus it was that the French public, whom Constable had earlier derided, telling Fisher (at the time of Arrowsmith's purchase of the picture) that he doubted whether the Parisians would be capable of understanding the beautiful simplicity of a country lane, came to recognize him as a great painter before his native countrymen.

He was to receive many commissions for paintings from France throughout the remainder of his life, but never accepted any of the offers made to him to visit the French capital, although he did give it very serious thought in the years immediately following his success at the Salon.

For most of the summer of 1824, he was constantly travelling to and from Brighton. While in London, he kept a charming little diary full of trivialities, such as the details of a quarrel between pigeons, and that the cats had knocked over some flowerpots, even what food he and Johnny Dunthorne had eaten. This diary was sent, in weekly serials, to Maria at Brighton, where the fresh, bracing sea air seemed to revive her ailing spirits and body.

Journeying to the south coast resort in September, Constable found several things of interest to him, and, naturally, made sketches of them. Most of these were fishermen's implements on the beach, and, just as he had, years earlier, recorded the agricultural tools used by the Suffolk farmers, so he now sketched these items.

Despite his abhorrence for Brighton, Constable was to come to admire it, albeit grudgingly, and derived sufficient inspiration from it to make it the subject of several paintings over the years he was there. It was also the choice of seaside resort when John Charles was fairly seriously ill some time later and needed sea air to aid his recuperation.

Meanwhile, the artist had immersed himself in his next six-foot canvas, which he was hastily preparing — with its attendent sketches — in time for the 1825 Academy. It was entitled *The Leaping Horse** and has come to be regarded, by many critics, as Constable's best picture. Certainly it was the most complex, and he seems to have had many doubts about it throughout its creation. It had been started in September, and several small studies preceded the first full-size sketch. Leslie, at the time, thought that Constable had intended the sketch to be the final picture but had become disillusioned with it and proceeded to a new canvas. This belief can be discounted by our knowledge of Constable's methods insofar as full-size sketches were concerned. (Leslie might not have been aware of any full-size sketches for other paintings, because some of them were not discovered until after the painter's death.) Many alterations were made by Constable, both in the time it was on his easel prior to the Academy and after it was returned unsold, as were so many of his now-famous pictures. His work on it was disturbed several times — Maria was in the final stages of another difficult pregnancy (Emily, their fifth child was born on March 29); Didot, a Paris dealer, arrived and ordered three paintings; and on May 8, immediately prior to the opening of the Academy, Bishop Fisher died.

The painting was sent off unfinished, its author wishing he could have spent a further three weeks on it prior to exhibition, for he realized that he had, with this picture, reached the zenith of his achievement, and it was partly the knowledge of this that caused him so much anxiety.

The subject of the picture is a further representation of rural East Anglian life, in this case one of the barge horses jumping one of the gates at varying intervals along the towpaths. The Suffolk horses were magnificent animals and had harnesses and collars with colorful plumage. The composition is full of the lifeblood of a Suffolk river: barges, the horse, the river itself, tree stumps, willows, and the distant church and footbridge. The scene itself does not truly reflect an exact spot on the river Stour, but is a collection of items from earlier sketchbooks. It was his attempt to produce a very full painting that caused Constable to make so many alterations to the painting.

At least two full-size sketches were made, as well as several smaller ones, before the final canvas was placed on his easel. The brushwork in the final picture — now in the Royal Academy in London — is magnificent; the strokes are short yet definite, with just the right amount of blending to dispel any clinical atmosphere; the reflections on the surface of the water look genuine, as do the shadows cast by the tree to the left, and the willow stump and old timbers look to be warped and weather-worn. The moor-hen frightened from her nest is also worth very careful study, not perhaps for its ornithological detail but for its character and attitude as it takes flight.

During the winter, when Constable had been working on *The Leaping Horse*, Fisher had attempted to put him off this work, suggesting that he should vary his style and pay more attention to contemporary public taste, but the painter retorted that he felt duty-bound to continue with his work in this style as he

---

* See p. 59.

THE CORNFIELD, 1826. Oil on canvas, 56¼″ × 48″ (113 × 122 cm)
The National Gallery, London

VALE OF DEDHAM, 1828. Oil on canvas, 57⅛″ × 48″ (145 × 122 cm)
National Galleries of Scotland, Edinburgh

The Beach at Brighton, 1824. Drawing, 7" × 12¾" (17.8 × 32.5 cm)
The British Museum, London

WATERLOO BRIDGE, 1824. Oil on canvas, $21^{11}/_{16}'' \times 30^{11}/_{16}''$ (55 × 77.9 cm)
Cincinnati Art Museum. Gift of Mary Hanna

Harnham Bridge, 1820. Drawing, 6⅛″ × 9″ (15.5 × 22.8 cm)
The British Museum

PARHAM MILL, GILLINGHAM, c. 1826. Oil on canvas, 19¾″ × 23¾″ (50.1 × 60.3 cm)
Yale Center for British Art, New Haven, Conn. Paul Mellon Collection

CHAIN PIER, BRIGHTON, 1827. Oil on canvas, 50″ × 72¾″ (127 × 184.8 cm)
The Tate Gallery, London

HADLEIGH CASTLE, THE MOUTH OF THE THAMES, MORNING AFTER A STORMY NIGHT, 1829
Oil on canvas, 48″ × 64¾″ (122 × 164.5 cm)
Yale Center for British Art, New Haven, Conn. Paul Mellon Collection

Water Lane, Stratford St. Mary, October 4, 1827
Pencil and grey wash, 13" × 8⅞" (33 × 22.4 cm)
Victoria and Albert Museum, London
◁

Water Lane, Stratford St. Mary, October 1827
Pen and grey wash, with touches of pencil and bistre, 8⅞" × 13"   (22.4 × 33.1 cm)
Victoria and Albert Museum, London

LANDSCAPE – HAMPSTEAD HEATH, c. 1830. Oil on canvas, 12⅞″ × 19¾″ (32.7 × 50 cm)
Yale University Art Gallery, New Haven, Conn.
Bequest of Blanche Barclay for the George C. Barclay Collection

VIEW AT HAMPSTEAD, LOOKING TOWARDS LONDON, December 7, 1833
Watercolor, 4½″ × 7½″ (11.5 × 19 cm). Victoria and Albert Museum, London

74

STOKE POGES CHURCH, July 1833. Watercolor, 5¼″ × 7¾″ (13.3 × 19.8 cm)
Victoria and Albert Museum, London

WATER-MEADOWS NEAR SALISBURY, 1830. Oil on canvas, 18″ × 21¾″ (45.7 × 55.3 cm)
Victoria and Albert Museum, London

Old Sarum, 1834. Watercolor, 11⅞″ × 19⅛″ (30 × 48.7 cm)
Victoria and Albert Museum, London

had gone a certain way along a difficult road and must finish, rather than wander off at a tangent and make no real progress. Technically, *The Leaping Horse* was his most complex picture, and it is most certainly worth examining closely if we are to fully comprehend what Constable was trying to say in his art.

There were further anxieties that year, for John Charles was still not in the best of health. His father worried constantly about him and could not paint calmly until the boy recovered a little following further convalescence at Brighton, enabling Constable to write to John Fisher on September 10: « I am now quietly at my easel again; I find it a cure for all ills. »

The family remained in Brighton throughout the year, to be joined by the painter on Christmas Eve. Maria was still terribly weak, and although Constable's love for her never wained, her continual ill-health was becoming a strain on him, thus restricting his painting. He was, at the time, very busy, with plenty of commissions on hand, some of which he had already been paid for. There was, at this time, no cause for anxiety over financial matters.

He had again taken up his *Waterloo Bridge** during November of 1825, planning to submit it for the Academy the following spring, but discarded it yet again on the advice of C. R. Leslie, who proposed a further Suffolk scene. So it was to the East Anglian countryside that he again turned.

As a boy he had walked to school every day to Dr. Grimwood's establishment at Dedham, and he had, naturally, taken the same route each day, across the fields and along a lane leading down to the village. During his tenacious sketching tours of 1813 and 1814, when his love for Maria was being hampered, he had returned to this lane and sat and sketched. Looking back on his sketchbooks, he now revisualized the scene, from the top of the hill, the tower of Dedham Church in the distance. He then proceeded to invent the scene as we know it from his painting *The Cornfield.***

It is an amazing hodge-podge of items from his earlier sketches and some of his paintings. The view as portrayed does not and did not exist; the church, for example, is not to be seen from that spot, but Constable decided that a certain amount of poetic licence was permissible (as he had, incidentally, in *The Leaping Horse* which also contains some topographical inaccuracies) and set to work to create a picture, though he intended it to be a true description of a typical country lane and not eye salve. The boy drinking from the stream had first appeared in a sketch in 1810; the plow, the broken gate, and the dog came from the 1814 sketchbook.

He went to great lengths to get the vegetation right, calling on the assistance of a Brighton botanist for true descriptions of the types of plants that would be growing in June and where they would grow; also whether they would be suitable food for the animals feeding on them in the left foreground. Despite his botanical accuracy and his artistic or poetic licence, *The Cornfield* failed to sell, despite a vigorous campaign by its painter to find a buyer. It was exhibited seven times that year alone, but still remained unsold at his death, shortly after which a group of admirers, including Wordsworth and Faraday, subscribed three hundred guineas between them in order to present the picture to the nation — the first Constable to be so owned. The year ended with another addition to the Constable household, Alfred Abram, born on November 14, some weeks prematurely, and the painter decided that his quiver was full. Maria seems to have had similar sentiments after the birth of her fourth child. She was very slow to recover from this pregnancy, now growing constantly weaker, which again filled her husband with anxiety. During the winter he decided that his family ought to move out of London, and looked toward the more pollution-free atmosphere of Hampstead.

The search for a permanent home took several months, but at last, in early summer, a suitable property was found, and the family moved into number 6 Well Walk, Hampstead, on August 26. The painter then took his two oldest sons down to Flatford for a short vacation. They had a marvelous time, fishing from the banks of the many rivers and streams, riding the still-busy barges and visiting relatives and old friends.

Earlier that year, Constable had been applauded by The Times as « unquestionably the first landscape painter of the day » in reviewing his paintings at the Academy, the most important of which was his *Chain Pier, Brighton.**** He had made many pencil and oil sketches of Brighton, but this one was the only painting that could be regarded as a major effort. We have mentioned that he abhorred Brighton, but that he found sufficient interest there to sketch; this antithesis could, perhaps, be explained by the very nature of his addiction to sketching whatever happened to be in front of him at any time.

---

* See p. 65.   ** See p. 62.   *** See p. 68.

LITTLEHAMPTON STORMY, 1835.   Watercolor, 4³⁄₈″ × 7¹⁄₄″ (11.4 × 18.5 cm)
British Museum, London. Reproduced by courtesy of the Trustees of the British Museum

VIEW IN THE GROUNDS OF ARUNDEL CASTLE, 1835
Pencil and watercolor, 4½″ × 7⅜″ (11.5 × 18.8 cm). Victoria and Albert Museum, London

80

The *Chain Pier* was another of Constable's pictures that failed to sell, only finding a buyer in the posthumous auction of his works. Turner completed a picture of the *Chain Pier* at about the same time, and although his painting is not reproduced in this book, it is worth studying alongside the Constable version to see the differences in their styles at this point in their respective careers. By mid-October Constable was back in Hampstead, preparing his paintings for the 1828 Academy, one of which was to be his *Dedham Vale*. John Fisher came to stay for ten days just before Christmas, but had to return to Dorset for the festive season as it was for him — as for most clergy then and now — a busy time of year.

Maria's health had been slightly improved by the final stages of yet another pregnancy, with its increased blood pressure, but she began to fail again soon after the birth of her seventh child, Lionell, on January 2. Her feeble constitution was pushed to the limit by the death of her father, Charles Bicknell, on March 9. He had been an apoplectic for years, and his continuing niggardliness over money throughout his last years had meant that his daughter had had to struggle. True, Constable should have been able to support his family, but we must remember that familial traditions one hundred and fifty years ago were rather different from those we acknowledge today.

Mr. Bicknell's death did benefit the Constable family financially, by a considerable amount, and meant that Constable could again stand before his easel free of all anxiety about money. Instead, there was to be anxiety over Maria's health and about that of the newly born Lionell. The painter took the entire family to the seaside again, hoping that the fresh air would heal Maria's lungs. This time, however, they were beyond repair. Pulmonary tuberculosis had taken its cruel grip of her, slowly but inexorably draining the life from her frail body.

They returned to Hampstead in September, and it was now plainly obvious that Maria would not see another Christmas. Fisher was called for, but was unable to come, having important diocesan matters to attend to in Dorset. Leslie called in early November, and although Constable was happy in Maria's presence, before he left the house, the painter took him into another room, grasped his hand, and burst into tears without saying a word. On Sunday, November 23, 1828, Maria Constable died, her feeble lungs finally collapsing under the strain of the disease that had afflicted her throughout her life. She was buried in a simple tomb at Hampstead Parish Church.

THE LAST YEARS, 1828–1837

«The face of the world is totally changed for me,» he told his brother Golding on December 19 — and it was true. The happiness he had waited so long for had been short-lived, and a deep sense of gloom settled upon him. He moved out of the Hampstead home, taking his children, one of whom was less than a year old, back to Charlotte Street, and it was only for the children that he carried on. Desolation pervaded his soul, and his art, from this time, takes on an angrier, depressive nature.

Shortly before Maria's death, and at a time when he knew she was dying, he had commenced work on a full-size sketch of *Hadleigh Castle*,* taking notes from the sketches he had made on a visit there in 1814, at a time when marriage looked anything but certain. Exactly why he returned to this subject at that precise time is uncertain, but he must have experienced some deep emotional reminiscence linking it with his love for Maria. This was to be the last picture for which he would make a full-size sketch. While at work on the painting itself, on the evening of February 10, 1829, Turner called on him. A year previously, when Constable was canvasing support for the Academy elections, Turner had received him at the door of his house, a clear indication of his forthcoming lack of support for Constable in the elections, as well as a sign of extreme impoliteness. But now it was Turner who bore the tidings that Constable had, that very evening, been finally elected a full member of the Academy, albeit only by one vote over his rival.

His sense of pride at finally being appointed a Royal Academician did little to dispel his prevailing grief. In fact, it depressed him further, as he considered it to be nothing more than a sop by the high-minded academicians to compensate him for his loss. His visit to the president of the Royal Academy, Sir Thomas Lawrence, to be formally advised of his appointment, confirmed this view, as Sir Thomas

---

* See p. 69.

lectured him sternly on the inadvisability of continuing with landscapes, and lost no opportunity to remind him how fortunate he was to have been elected when there were so many good painters around!

Constable had been exhibiting at the Academy for twenty-seven years, sometimes with a good reception, sometimes a bad one, more often than not with indifference; but this year, when he was, as a full Academician, spared the necessity of submitting works for approval, he was treated with disdain. During the days allotted to the painters to retouch their work after it had been hung, one rival painter, Chantry, snatched Constable's palette from him and painted out much of the foreground of *Hadleigh Castle* which Constable had painstakingly put in to give the impression of early morning dew. There was insufficient time to repair it, and so the picture was exhibited in its vandalized state — and came in for much criticism. The dark, thundery clouds above the desolate, marshy estuary tell more about Constable's mood at the time than any words.

Painting now, once again, took on the nature of therapy for Constable; for a while he took the family back to Hampstead, making several studies of the Heath. In early July he took the two oldest children, John and Minna, to Salisbury to stay with the Fishers, leaving the other children in the secure, tender care of their nurse, Miss Roberts, and the family housekeeper, Mrs. Savage, whose nature, according to her employer, was anything but that inferred by her name.

The countryside and gentle charm of the Wessex cathedral city soothed him, and he again found sufficient enthusiasm to put pencil to paper, sketching hastily but carefully in and around Salisbury.

Constable returned to London on July 28, refreshed and newly enthused, happy to see his two oldest children once again enjoying the family life with the Fishers after their grievous loss. Indeed, Minna seemed so happy that, with her father's blessing, she remained in Wessex until November, when Constable journeyed to Salisbury to collect her. Ironically, that was the last time Constable was to see the archdeacon, now advanced in years like the painter himself. Fisher also needed money and asked Constable to buy back both *The White Horse* and *Salisbury Cathedral*. The painter did so.

During 1829 Constable had decided that it would now be appropriate to have some prints made of some of his paintings in order that they might be enjoyed by a wider audience. At that time, all paintings for reproduction had to be engraved by an artistic hand, as there were none of today's modern photographic or printing machines. Thus Constable selected a Northamptonshire engraver, David Lucas, the son of a farmer and, like Constable, a keen student of the countryside. Lucas had, himself, painted several landscapes before turning to framing and engraving. Throughout 1829 and the first half of 1830, Lucas labored on his engravings, suffering much scathing criticism from Constable the whole time. Like almost any artisan, Constable could not bear the thought that someone else could do sufficient justice to his work in the process of copying it. Lucas also bore the brunt of Constable's restlessness, brought on by a combination of grief and the passage of years. Ill-health, partly caused by anxiety over Lucas's work, only added to Constable's misery at the time.

By July 1830, the first volume of the prints was ready for publication, and Constable had to give much time to the matters arising from that event. Young John had again been seriously ill, and had to return to stay with friends at Brighton, but had returned to Hampstead by November, in time for all the family to celebrate Christmas together.

Constable spent some time during that winter at work on his Academy picture for the 1831 Exhibition, although his work on it was interrupted many times by illness.

Another, and rather unusual activity, took up considerable time during January and February, his having been appointed Life Visitor at the Academy. The duties of the Visitor were to instruct the students, and it is somewhat surprising that Constable did this as his life drawing had never been exceptional, but he threw himself into his duties with conviction if not with enthusiasm.

In his Academy picture, *Salisbury Cathedral from the Meadows*, now in the collection of Lord Ashton of Hyde, Constable's melancholy mood is evident. The keynote of the picture is the rainbow, arcing down from the dark, foreboding storm clouds. Had Bishop Fisher lived to see this painting, he would, surely, have been shocked at the thundery aspect. He was, we recall, most disturbed at the light cloud cover in the original *Salisbury Cathedral* of 1823. The painter seems to have been overly concerned with the picture, even after the Exhibition. It became one of the works that Lucas was to engrave for publication, and Constable followed its progress carefully. He carried out a considerable amount of work on the picture after it had been first exhibited, probably, once again, proving that he relied enormously on the value of sentiment in his work. The bishop had been a good friend, as was his nephew, Archdeacon Fisher — though he too was now in poor health — and Salisbury obviously held

Englefield House, Berkshire (Detail), August 1832
Pencil, 11⅛″ × 8⅞″ (28.4 × 22.3 cm)
Victoria and Albert Museum, London

Willy Lott's House, c. 1812. Drawing, 8" × 11¼" (20.5 × 28.6 cm)
Courtauld Institute Galleries, London

THE VALLEY FARM, 1835. Oil on canvas, 58½″ × 49½″ (149 × 126 cm). The Tate Gallery, London

many memories for Constable. Yet here he is portraying the glorius cathedral under a cloud, troubled by storms, and the suggestion that this was a reflection of his own outlook on life at that time must be taken seriously. The picture was savagely attacked in The Guardian, its painter held up to ridicule.

For much of the summer Constable was again in Suffolk, this time without the boys but with his three daughters, but he had to return to the capital to attend a Royal Academy Committee meeting in July and stayed on to attend the coronation of William IV. As a Royal Academician, he was entitled to a seat in Westminster Abbey for the occasion. He enjoyed the spectacle. In a very colorful letter to Leslie, he described how he had remained in his place for the full eleven hours of the ceremony, and had a fine view as the crown was placed on the head of the king and then one on the head of Queen Adelaide. The moment the king was crowned, all the peers of the realm placed replica crowns on their own heads and cried out «God Save the King,» after which trumpets sounded a fanfare and bands began to play, the choirs singing joyful anthems of thanksgiving.

The magnificent colors and the spectacle must have excited his artist's eye, but he made no effort to reproduce the scene in a painting. It certainly would have made a marvelous subject and could have done much to increase his popularity, particularly with the Establishment.

Instead, he turned again to a painting that was colorful, one which he had worked on several times previously, but had, on the advice of friends, put aside each time in order to paint a Suffolk landscape. This was the *Waterloo Bridge** he had started about ten years earlier.

Waterloo Bridge had been opened on June 18, 1817, by the Prince Regent to commemorate the second anniversary of the Battle of Waterloo, and it was one of the most spectacular pageants Londoners had witnessed. Among them was the much younger Constable. Exactly why he was so long in completing it is uncertain. It is not a great painting, particularly when viewed beside one of Canaletto's fine London scenes. In fact, according to Constable, it never was completely finished. Probably, the spectacle of the coronation revived his enthusiasm for this colorful picture, but he had many distractions during the winter of 1831–1832, not least of which was a very bad attack of rheumatism that left him without the use of his right hand for several weeks during which time he could neither paint nor write.

At the end of February he told Lucas that he was «dashing away at the great London . . . I may as well produce this abortion as another — for who cares for landscape?» a statement that seems to indicate his still depressed state. It was unfortunate that the painting, full of bright colors even if unfinished, was hung next to Turner's *Helvoetsluys*, a gray picture with very little color. During the days allowed for retouching and final varnishing, Turner apparently came in, looked at the two paintings hanging together, then suddenly took up his palette and daubed a blob of red lead in the middle of his sea. This was so startling in an otherwise colorless painting that it completely stole the limelight from the Constable.

In the summer Archdeacon Fisher, who had been seriously ill during the last winter, was taken to Boulogne in an attempt to improve his health, but in vain, for, on the afternoon of Friday, August 24, he was seized with violent spasms and was dead within twenty-four hours. Within a few months, his faithful friend and assistant, young John Dunthorne, died of a heart attack on November 2. Constable went down to Suffolk to attend Dunthorne's funeral on a cold, damp November morning, the church bells tolling mournfully through the mist, acknowledging yet again the finality of death.

He returned sadly to London and decided to take the children to Hampstead for the winter. The irrepressible joyfulness of his sons and daughters rekindled his spirits, and he set to work on the pictures he planned to show at the 1833 Academy. There were several, including the charming *Cottage in a Cornfield*, which he had earlier painted but now retouched. The liveliness of this little picture points to it having been painted years earlier, for it contains none of the darkness that afflicted his later years. A similar painting had been shown in 1817.

His two major pictures were *Englefield House,*** and *The Cenotaph.*** The former was completed through a commission for the owner of the House, Benyon de Beovoir, who was the High Sheriff of Berkshire. Constable never liked painting architectural detail, unless, as in the case of Salisbury, it held for him sentimental memories, but in his earlier years he had accepted many commissions for house portraits primarily for the money they brought in. It seems that de Beovoir had asked for a painting of his house several years earlier, but it was only now that Constable found the time to complete it. It was, as he told Leslie, a chore, and he kept putting it aside to start work on new paintings, one of which was *The Cenotaph*. On the grounds of Coleorton Hall, the home of Sir George Beaumont, had been erected a monument to the

---

* See p. 65.   ** See drawing p. 83.   *** See p. 88.

memory of Sir Joshua Reynolds, and this picture would have been, for Constable, a labor of love, or at least of respect, both for Reynolds and for Sir George. Unfortunately, he did not have time to complete the painting for that year's Academy and submitted instead some older pictures.

Englefield House came in for much criticism, as being not a painting but an architectural exhibit, in bad taste, poorly painted, and various other none too complimentary comments.

Always a good and attentive father, Constable never failed to take the time to give some of his many children a holiday, and during the summer of 1833 he took the two oldest boys, John and Charles, to Suffolk for three happy weeks spent scouring the woods for fossils, fishing the abundant streams, and sketching in the peace of the countryside.

Constable had, a few years previously, employed the services of a tutor to avoid having to send the boys away to school, but the time had now come when their education needed further advancement, and so their father found them a comfortable school in Folkestone on the Kent coast. He accompanied them both there in September, after their return from Suffolk, and stayed with them a few days while they settled into their new surroundings.

In mid-October, young John suffered a nasty fall, injuring his spine, and on hearing of the accident Constable took the first available coach down to Kent to be with his son. Luckily, the injury was not as serious as had first been thought, so Constable was able to travel back to London by the end of the month. The coach was cold and drafty, and once again the dampness and evils of winter afflicted him. He caught a severe cold, was laid low, and was unable to paint for several weeks, rheumatic fever once again putting his right hand out of action.

He had been saddened by the departure, in September, of his friend and near-neighbor at Hampstead, C. R. Leslie, who had, together with his family, sailed for America to take up a teaching post at West Point. The two men had kept in touch, writing often to each other, and in one of Constable's letters, dated January 20, 1834, he told Leslie that he was only just recovering from the fever, and could now, once more, paint, but only with great pain. Finding it so difficult to paint, he resorted to the less taxing medium of watercolors to paint *Old Sarum.* *

Sarum had once been a fine town, built in Roman times on a mound not far from the present-day city of Salisbury. By the eighteenth century it was nothing more than a deserted ruin, wild, desolate, silent. Again it is interesting and very sad to note that Constable chose this as subject matter — a once-fine city, in which the earliest English parliaments met, now reduced to a lonely, windswept heap of rubble. In the notes he composed to accompany the plate of *Old Sarum* in the *English Landscapes* that Lucas was engraving, he reiterated the feelings that had doubtless possessed him while painting it — « wild, desolate and dreary; contrasts strongly with its former greatness.»

The coming of spring brought some relief from the pain and gloom of the winter, and he was much cheered by the news that Leslie was returning to England that summer, having decided not to settle in America. By September Constable had once again met his old friend, and they spent some time together at Petworth in Sussex. Constable had, some years earlier, struck up a friendship with a brewer from Arundel, who, although he went by the name of George Constable, was not related to the painter. While at Petworth, Constable again paid a visit to his namesake and made several drawings of the castle at Arundel.

A further painting of Willy Lott's house was made for the 1835 Academy, and was purchased for three hundred pounds several weeks before the exhibition, and well before it was finished. The purchaser was the collector Robert Vernon, who had called on Constable and took an instant liking to the *Valley Farm.* ** He had to wait some time for it though, as Constable carried out further work on it, improving it little by little, up to October of that year. On September 8, Constable said a sad farewell to his son Charles, as he boarded the East Indiaman «Buckinghamshire» about to set sail for Bombay. Charles had taken a liking to the sea some years earlier, and it had always been his ambition to sail. Although Constable was upset and concerned about his son setting forth upon the treacherous waters, he did nothing to discourage him. Charles was a dreamy boy, full of bright ideas about the wonder of life, unaware of some of the hazards that were to be encountered along the way.

John, the oldest boy, was rather different, more like his father in his youth. He was shy to the point of being timid, had immaculate manners, and was a gentle, but dedicated scholar. He was studying Greek, Latin, chemistry and anatomy at the Royal Institution (one of his teachers was Professor Michael Faraday) before going to Cambridge to take Holy Orders.

---

* See p. 77.   ** See p. 85.

THE CENOTAPH, 1836. Oil on canvas, 52″ × 42¾″ (132 × 111 cm). The National Gallery, London

The Royal Academy had, for some time, been considering a move from its Somerset House abode, and the 1836 Exhibition was to be the last at that place. Constable took up, again, *The Cenotaph*, telling George Constable in a letter that he wanted to see the names of Reynolds and Beaumont in the catalogue for the last Somerset House Exhibition. In the catalogue Constable included the inscription on the monument, which was composed by the poet Wordsworth, but which is not legible on the painting, save for the name «Reynolds.»

The watercolor of *Stonehenge** was also shown at that year's Exhibition.

On August 30 the «Buckinghamshire» docked, home from her long voyage to India. Constable was on the dockside to greet his son, now grown into a young man, stouter, surer, maturer. The homecoming was short, for Charles was to leave again for a voyage to China on November 27. During October the winter had set in, with early snows covering most of the country, being driven into huge drifts by the icy gales, and leaving, in its wake, thousands of dead sheep and cattle, stranded on the freezing hills.

Charles's ship was severely pounded in the Channel, and was driven into port on the south coast for several days until the winds abated sufficiently for it to make its way. Constable had deep misgivings about the journey, unsure whether he would see his son again, for the duration of the voyage would be at least two years.

Constable set to work that winter on a painting of Arundel Mill and Castle which, he informed George Constable, would be his best painting ever. The setting enchanted him and he tackled the picture with a genuine affection, with none of the gloomy depression of earlier years. The Academy was in the process of moving to its new building in Trafalgar Square (which now houses the National Gallery), and the painter wanted to ensure that his first exhibit in the new home would be a good one.

He was again, that winter, the Life Visitor at the Academy, and had the honor to take the last Life Class ever held in Somerset House on Saturday, evening March 25. He concluded the lesson, made a short speech, and was heartily cheered by the students.

The following Thursday he went to a meeting of the Royal Academy in its new home in Trafalgar Square. Although the night was bitterly cold, he insisted on walking home, accompanied by Leslie. As the two men walked along Oxford Street, a small girl on the opposite side of the street fell over and grazed her knee. Hearing her cry, Constable crossed over, picked her up, rubbed her knee better and gently soothed her, giving her a shilling for bread, as she was obviously from a very poor family. The two men walked on to the end of the street, then parted to go to their separate homes. It was to be the last time Leslie would see his old friend.

The following morning Constable worked on *Arundel Mill and Castle*** before going out, in the late afternoon, on an errand connected with a charity of which he was a director. He returned home around eight thirty in the evening, ate a hearty supper, and went to bed. Shortly before midnight, his son John Charles, coming home from the theater, heard his father call out in pain. He rushed to his room, shouted for the housekeeper, who sent next door for some brandy, and summoned a doctor.

Before the brandy could be brought up, John Constable died. The date was Friday, March 31, 1837.

A few days later Constable was buried, his simple coffin being carried by his brothers Abram and Golding, as it was laid to rest beside Maria in the tomb at Hampstead. John Charles was so upset that he could not attend the funeral — just as Constable had been unable to attend his mother's burial twenty-two years earlier.

The painter's son Charles did not learn of his father's death until four months later, when he read of it in a Bombay newspaper, where his ship had stopped on its journey east.

Little Minna, seventeen years old, now took upon herself the mantel of protector of the family; John went to Cambridge to read Theology at Jesus College.

In 1839 little Emily, just fourteen years old, contracted scarlet fever and died. Two years later John succumbed to the same disease and was laid in his grave. In November 1853, Alfred drowned in the Thames.

Today, Constable's paintings remain memorials to the great man who saw Nature in all Her glory and portrayed Her in that way. Tender, always gentle, a loving husband, an adoring and adored father, a dedicated friend, he retained throughout his sixty years his simple, country manners.

---

* See back cover. ** See p. 90.

Yet the monuments to him remain: Willy Lott's cottage still stands, now converted into an art education center; Flatford Mill still attracts many visitors. The barges, barge horses, and the locks are gone. So too is the gaiety of the harvests, replaced by efficient, but undignified machines.

But most of all, the countryside remains — not, perhaps, quite so placid or quiet as it was in Constable's day. But if we take the time we can still find the tiny gurgling brook, the silent woodland glade where we can sit, just as young John Constable sat, and admire the tranquillity of Nature in all her bounteous glory. Then we can understand what enthralled the young man who came to epitomize the genius of English landscape — John Constable.

ARUNDEL MILL AND CASTLE, 1837. Oil on canvas, 28½″ × 39½″ (72.4 × 100.3 cm)
The Todelo Museum of Art. Gift of Edward Drummond Libbey

1776. John Constable was born on June 11, in the Suffolk village of East Bergholt.

1792. Constable was introduced to Sir George Beaumont, who was to become a great influence on the painter.

1799. Enrolled as a probationary student at the Royal Academy in London.

1801. Painted his first commissioned picture — a view of Old Hall, East Bergholt.

1802. At the Royal Academy first exhibit.

1803. Journeyed down the Thames aboard the « Coutts » making many sketches of shipping and clouds.

1806. Exhibited a watercolor of the Battle of Trafalgar at the Royal Academy.

1809. Met and fell in love with Maria Bicknell.

1811. Visited Salisbury for the first time, meeting young John Fisher.

1813. In his frustration at being unable to marry Maria, he spent some time sketching furiously in East Anglia, filling a remarkable sketchbook.

1815. In May, his mother died, followed a few days later by Maria's mother.

1816. His father died, also in May. In October he finally married Maria.

1817. In February Maria suffered a miscarriage but gave birth to their first son in December. Constable exhibited *Flatford Mill* at the Academy.

1819. The first of his six-foot canvases, *The White Horse* was shown at the Academy. In November he was finally elected an Associate of the Royal Academy.

1820. *The Young Waltonians* his second large canvas, was shown.

1821. The most famous Constable picture was completed and shown at the Academy — *The Hay-Wain*. His third child was born in March.

1823. After a slight disagreement with Bishop Fisher, Constable exhibited his *Salisbury Cathedral* — with clouds.

1824. In an effort to aid Maria's health, the family went to Brighton, which Constable hated.

1825. *The Leaping Horse* was exhibited. Bishop Fisher died.

1826. *The Cornfield* was shown at the Academy.

1827. To escape the filth of London, the family moved to the cleaner air of Hampstead.

1828. Maria's health deteriorated even further after the birth of her seventh child in January, and she was laid in her tomb in November.

1829. Constable was finally elected a Royal Academician, just a few weeks after Maria's death.

1832. Two of his closest friends — Archdeacon John Fisher and John Dunthorne junior — died.

1836. At the last Royal Academy Exhibition at Somerset House, Constable exhibited *The Cenotaph* as a memorial to Sir Joshua Reynolds.

1837. On March 31, John Constable died.

SELECT BIBLIOGRAPHY

« *Memoirs of the Life of John Constable, R. A.* » by C. R. Leslie. First published in 1843, this work presents a great deal of information, as it contains many of the letters written by Constable to his friends. Leslie interspersed these letters with his own notes, and the book, which has appeared in many editions, is a most valuable guide to the understanding of Constable as a person. There are no illustrations. The most recent edition was issued in 1971, by Paul P. B. Minet.

« *Constable — the Natural Painter.* » by Graham Reynolds. This book (available in paperback) was first published in 1965 by Adams & Mackay Ltd. Graham Reynolds was, for many years, Keeper of the Constable Collection at the Victoria & Albert Museum in London — which contains the largest Constable collection in the world; this is a fairly short history of the painter and his development, although there are very few illustrations.

« *Catalogue of the Constable Collection in the V & A.* » by Graham Reynolds. This is a full catalogue, with illustrations, of every work in the V & A Constable Collection — 597 works in all.

« *John Constable's Correspondence.* » edited by R. B. Beckett. This is an invaluable work containing nearly all the letters Constable wrote or received throughout his life.

« *Constable* » by Basil Taylor, published by Phaidon. This well illustrated book contains a brief account of Constable's life, with descriptions of some of his paintings.

« *Constable Oil Sketches* » by John Baskett. This book contains thirty-two of Constable's lesser-known oil sketches, and a very brief description of the painter's style.

« *John Constable* » by Carlos Peacock, published in 1965. This book, reasonably well illustrated, partially in color, contains a description of Constable's style in relation to some of the influences upon him.

« *John Constable* » by Freda Constable, the wife of the painter's great-great-grandson. This book, published in 1975, contains much interesting material and a number of illustrations to highlight the text.

« *Constable* » Parris, Fleming-Williams & Shields. This book, well-illustrated, contains the full details of every picture included in the Tate Gallery's Bicentenary Exhibition of 1976 and is well worth studying.

ILLUSTRATIONS

Ann Constable 42

Archdeacon John Fisher 44

Arundel Castle (View in the Grounds of) . . 80

Arundel Mill and Castle 90

Autumnal Sunset 36

Barges on the Stour 35

Beach at Brighton (The) 64

Boat Building near Flatford Mill 22–23

Boat Passing a Lock 60

Bridge at Haddon 8

Cart and Horses 33

Cenotaph (The) 88

Chain Pier, Brighton 68

Cornfield (The) 62

Cumulus Clouds (Study for) 52

Dedham Church 25

East Bergholt Old Hall 5

Edensor 9

Elm Trees in Old Hall Park 54

Englefield House 83

Flatford Mill 27

Girl and Dog in a Landscape 7

Girl at a Window 14

Golding Constable 43

Hadleigh Castle 69

Hampstead (View at) 74

Hampstead Heath 73

Hampstead Heath (Landscape) 72

Harnham Bridge 66

Hay-Wain (The) 39

Hay-Wain (Study for the) 38

Head of a Girl in Profile 11

Keswick Lake 16

Lane near East Bergholt 34

Leaping Horse (The) 59

Leaping Horse (Study for the) 58

Life Study 31

Littlehampton Stormy 79

Man-O-War, Chatham 20

Maria Bicknell 41

Maria with two Children 40

Mill Stream (The) 26

Old Sarum 77

Overbury Hall 55

Parham Mill, Gillingham 67

Road near Dedham 13

Salisbury Cathedral 57

Salisbury Cathedral W. Door 56

Self-Portrait 29

Shipping in the Thames 21

St. Mary-ad-Murum Church 25

Stoke Poges Church 75

Stratocumulus Cloud 49

Two Gleaners 24

Vale of Dedham 63

Valley Farm (The) 85

View in Borrowdale 15

Water Lane, Stratford St. Mary 70, 71

Water-Meadows near Salisbury 76

Waterloo Bridge 65

Weymouth Bay 37

Willy Lott's House 84

We wish to thank the owners of the pictures reproduced herein,
as well as those collectors who did not want to have their names mentioned:

MUSEUMS

AUSTRALIA

National Gallery of Victoria, Melbourne.

FRANCE

Musée Bonnat, Bayonne.
Musée du Louvre, Cabinet des Dessins, Paris.

U. K.

The British Museum, London.
Colchester and Essex Museum.
Courtauld Institute Galleries, London.
Fitzwilliam Museum, Cambridge.
Ipswich Art Gallery and Museum.

The National Gallery, London.
National Portrait Gallery, London.
National Galleries of Scotland, Edinburgh.
The Royal Academy of Arts, London.
The Tate Gallery, London.
Victoria and Albert Museum, London.

U.S.A.

Cincinnati Art Museum.
Museum of Fine Arts, Boston.
The Frick Collection, New York.
The Toledo Museum of Art.
Yale Center for British Art.
Yale University Art Gallery.

PRIVATE COLLECTIONS

Thos. Agnew and Sons Ltd., London – Walter Morrison Picture Settlement, Sudeley Castle, Winchcombe, Cheltenham, Gloncestershire.